LEARNING OBJECTIVES FOR INDIVIDUALIZED INSTRUCTION

SCIENCE

Westinghouse Learning Press
Division of Westinghouse Learning Corporation

Library of Congress Card Catalog Number 75-23425

ISBN 0-88250-780-X (Softcover Edition)
ISBN 0-88250-775-3 (Hardcover Edition)

Text set in 10 point Zenith with display
lines in 13 point Goudy Heavyface

Cover design and art by Steven Jacobs Design,
Palo Alto, California

Editorial and production by Westinghouse
Learning Press, Sunnyvale, California

Composition by Typothetae, Palo Alto, California

Lithography by George Banta Company,
Menasha, Wisconsin

Contents

Objectives from the following Westinghouse Learning Press publications have been used or adapted with permission of the authors.

Biology: An Individualized Course
Robert N. Hurst, David H. McGaw, Kenneth H. Bush, Curtis L. Smiley

Earth Science: An Individualized Course
Joseph C. Gould, Charles J. Mott, N. Gerald Langford

Algebra: An Individualized Course
Ephraim G. Salins, Russell L. Fleury

American Government: An Individualized Course
Wallace P. Harrison

Sociology: An Individualized Course, First Edition and Revised Edition
Robert A. Butler

Psychology: An Individualized Course, First Edition and Revised Edition
Richard L. Morgan

Economics: An Individualized Course
Dayton Y. Roberts, Alfred J. Furnweger

English Composition: An Individualized Course, First Edition and Revised Edition
Benson R. Schulman

A Curse on Confusion: An Individualized Approach to Clear Writing
Lowell A. Draper

The Relevance of Patterns: An Individualized Approach to Writing Improvement
Lucille M. Thomas

The Relevance of Sound: An Individualized Approach to Phonetic and Structural Analysis
Frances Coolidge

The Relevance of Words: An Individualized Approach to Spelling
David J. Peterson

The Relevance of Listening: An Individualized Course
Harold D. Sartain

AC Circuits/DC Circuits: An Individualized Approach to Electronics
Paul E. Trejo

Toward Instructional Accountability: A Practical Guide to Educational Change
John E. Roueche, Barton R. Herrscher

Computer Programming: An Individualized Course in FORTRAN IV
Carl A. Grame, Daniel J. O'Donnell

Introduction

Westinghouse Learning Corporation has been involved for almost ten years in developing individualized instructional material for kindergarten, elementary school, high school, college, career training, and industry. Since objectives are a basic component of individualized learning, Westinghouse Learning Corporation has necessarily been a leader in formulating objectives.

With increasing demands for accountability in teaching, many teachers and instructors have found a need for objectives to use or to adapt for their courses. Others wanted guidelines so that they could develop their own objectives as they moved toward greater individualization and accountability in teaching.

This set of objectives has been produced to provide learning objectives for an age range quite different from the usual grade levels, particularly for the mature student, who may never have mastered objectives that are ordinarily covered in earlier years. The typical grade-level organization is not appropriate for these students, who may need some very basic elements but are nonetheless ready to explore the disciplines at a comparatively sophisticated level.

Most of these objectives have been used with students, particularly in classes that emphasize individualization as well as in learning centers and resource laboratories that concentrate on a diagnostic and remedial approach to basic skills.

Cognitive Levels

In the first Westinghouse Learning Corporation collection, *Behavioral Objectives,* the keying of objectives to cognitive levels based on Bloom's *Taxonomy of Educational Objectives, Cognitive Domain,* was so successful that this system has been used again, with some adaptations. Determining the cognitive level of objectives necessarily involves a degree of subjectivity, but every effort has been made to reduce subjectivity through use of a chart, listing the verbs that seem appropriate for behavior at the various cognitive levels. Often modifiers of these verbs have had to be added. Where questions arose regarding the cognitive level of the objectives in these volumes, the editors made judgments as to the actual performance involved, based on the following questions that help to define the six basic levels.

I. Are the students asked simply to repeat facts or show that they have memorized something?

II. Do students have to show understanding of the information presented?

III. Must students apply knowledge to a new situation (as in problem solving), or must they make predictions?

IV. Is it necessary to analyze and organize information?

V. Does the objective require combining and presenting information in a new or creative way?

VI. Do students have to draw together several cognitive levels in evaluating the material or in making judgments based on evaluation?

Using these six questions as the framework, the editors developed the chart on pages viii–ix, which lists verbs that have been used for each of the cognitive levels.

A major difficulty in assigning levels arises from the confusion between the *kinds* of cognitive activity and the *content* associated with that activity. For example, to the student in medical school, a large amount of cognitive activity may be of the kind that is often referred to as the lowest level, memorization. Anatomical terms, drug dosages, symptoms, and treatments must be memorized. The content level of this activity is extremely high, but the activity itself remains at level I. A conscious effort has been made in this collection to present objectives that cover a broad spectrum of cognitive levels and content. It is up to the user of these books to transform a given objective to meet either the content or the cognitive level that is appropriate for a particular unit of instruction.

Organization

Beyond the major divisions into four volumes—Language Arts, Mathematics, Science, and Social Science—a broad set of subject classifications has been used. No attempt has been made to provide comprehensive subject coverage, and many objectives in one category are also applicable to another. The comprehensive index provides cross referencing. Although there are subject subdivisions, there is no grade-level designation. When any text is made up of small parts, the constraints of print mean that each item has a fixed position on a page and within a volume—a position that establishes a sequential relationship regardless of whether such a relationship is logical or intentional. Since objectives may potentially be sequenced in many ways, it is important to understand that the arrangement of this collection is not intended to suggest any prescriptive order. In the sections emphasizing skills, there is some natural sequence based on the cumulative nature of some skills, but in subject areas topics may be presented in almost any order.

In *Learning Objectives for Individualized Instruction,* terminal objectives have been established to provide appropriate learning segments. These terminal objectives are numbered and printed in boldface.

Subobjectives, which may be called transitional or enabling objectives, contribute to the mastery of a terminal objective. These transitional objectives may appear as part of more than one terminal objective. Transitional objectives and terminal objectives are both assigned cognitive levels; transitional objectives are never given a higher cognitive level than the terminal objectives with which they are associated.

The Numbering System

Because many instructors wish to use the computer for storage and retrieval of objectives and related test items, each terminal objective has been given a numerical designator. These numbers have been set up as follows. The two digits at the far left indicate a major area: 01, Language Arts; 02, Mathematics; 03, Social Science; 04, Science. Career areas and other major areas can be added, up to 99. The three middle digits have been reserved for subject areas; in this collection numbers have been assigned to subject areas at intervals of five to allow for interpolation of such other subjects as an instructor finds appropriate. The three digits on the right in the numerical designator signify terminal objectives; these have also been spaced at intervals of five so that others may be inserted.

Since courses have not yet been developed in all subject areas, some disciplines are not covered in this collection and there has been no effort to make coverage complete within a subject area. This collection is designed to encourage the instructor to use these volumes as guidelines rather than as a definite set. Every instructor should feel free to add, subtract, and adapt objectives to meet individual, class, and institutional needs.

Levels of Learning Objectives

I KNOWLEDGE	II COMPREHENSION	III APPLICATION
Emphasis: Recall	*Emphasis:* Grasp of meaning, intent, or relationship	*Emphasis:* Applying appropriate principles or generalizations
choose from a list (judgment not involved) define (give a dictionary definition) fill in the blank (or complete) follow directions identify indicate label list locate (on a map or a given document) match name select (judgment not involved)	classify define (in student's own words) describe explain express in other terms find (as in math) measure paraphrase put in order recognize rewrite simplify suggest summarize trace (on a map, chart, etc.) *Math* add (find the sum) balance calculate compute (using a given formula) divide (find the quotient) factor find square root or raise to power multiply (find the product) perform operations on numbers subtract (find the difference)	apply collect information (supply correct equation or formula) compute construct convert (in math) draw determine (calculate) demonstrate derive differentiate between discuss distinguish between expand express in a discussion estimate find (implies investigation) interpret investigate illustrate (give examples not previously specified) graph keep records locate (information) make participate perform (except in math or in public) plan predict (from known factors) prepare present prove (in math) solve (problems expressed in words) use trace (development, history, process) translate

Levels of Learning Objectives (continued)

IV ANALYSIS	V SYNTHESIS	VI EVALUATION
Emphasis: Breaking into constituent parts and detecting relationships of the parts and the way they are organized and organizing material according to a coherent pattern	*Emphasis:* Putting together elements or parts to form a whole that reflects originality	*Emphasis:* On values, making qualitative or quantitative judgment, using criteria from internal or external sources and standards
analyze compare and contrast criticize debate deduce determine differentiate between (by analysis) draw conclusions formulate form generalizations make inferences organize relate (show relationships)	combine and organize design devise develop perform (in public) produce present (an original report or work) write (an original composition)	choose (based on evaluation) decide evaluate judge make a decision

This collection would not be possible without the cooperation of the following:

Science: Robert N. Hurst, Purdue University, Lafayette, Indiana; Kenneth H. Bush, David H. McGaw, and Curtis L. Smiley, West Lafayette High School, West Lafayette, Indiana; Joseph C. Gould, Charles J. Mott, and N. Gerald Langford, St. Petersburg Junior College, Clearwater, Florida; Miles H. Anderson, University of California, Los Angeles, California; Paul E. Trejo, De Anza College, Cupertino, California

Mathematics: Ephraim G. Salins, Montgomery College, Takoma Park, Maryland; Russell L. Fleury, University of Maryland, College Park, Maryland; Carl A. Grame and Daniel J. O'Donnell, De Anza College, Cupertino, California

Social Science: Wallace P. Harrison, Los Angeles Pierce College, Los Angeles, California; Robert A. Butler, Louisburg College, Louisburg, North Carolina; Richard L. Morgan, Mitchell College, Statesville, North Carolina; Dayton Y. Roberts, Texas Tech University, Lubbock, Texas; Alfred J. Furnweger, Santa Fe Community College, Gainesville, Florida; John E. Roueche, University of Texas, Austin, Texas; Barton R. Herrscher, College Associates, Austin, Texas; Rita and Stuart Johnson, School of Medicine, University of North Carolina, Chapel Hill, North Carolina; Marcia H. Perlstein, Opportunity II High School, San Francisco, California

Language Arts: Benson R. Schulman, Los Angeles Pierce College, Los Angeles, California; Lowell A. Draper, Modesto Community College, Modesto, California; Lucille M. Thomas, Grand Rapids Junior College, Grand Rapids, Michigan; Frances Coolidge, De Anza College, Cupertino, California; David J. Peterson, San Jose Unified School District, San Jose, California; Harold D. Sartain, Des Moines Area Community College, Ankeny, Iowa

Further acknowledgment is made to all who participated in developing objectives for Project PLAN* and *Behavioral Objectives: A Guide to Individualizing Learning.*

The Editors
Westinghouse Learning Press
Sunnyvale, California
15 September 1975

SCIENCE

Biology

04-005-005   **Support or reject, using the experimental designs of Stanley Miller and Sidney Fox, the heterotroph hypothesis regarding a possible sequence of events that might have produced the first polypeptides.   VI**

Identify the one ingredient most necessary for life to have originated on Earth.   I

State reasons both for and against the heterotroph and autotroph hypotheses for the origin of life.   II

Identify the gases and the major sources of energy that were present in the primitive atmosphere of our planet.   I

Present a sequence of events that may have taken place on the primitive Earth to lead to the formation of complex organic molecules and subsequently to life.   II

04-005-010   **Differentiate between theories that explain the geologic record of life in the past and those explaining the origin of life.   IV**

Describe the sediment-dating and radioactive-clock methods of dating fossils.   II

Given a chart that illustrates evolutionary relationships of organisms, trace the common ancestors of different organisms.   II

Summarize the factors that eventually led to a decline in the dominance of amphibians and reptiles and to an increase in the dominance of mammals.   II

04-005-015   **Compare examples of straight-line, divergent, and convergent evolution.   VI**

Identify a weakness in Darwin's theory of evolution.   I

Recognize the Lamarckian theory of evolution, and describe an experiment that tests this hypothesis.   II

Given three observations Darwin made about evolution, draw three conclusions he could have made. IV

Recognize evidence that supports Darwin's theory of evolution. II

Order chronologically four genera of equus that appear in evolutionary history. II

Recognize the relationship of mutation and isolation to Darwin's theory of evolution. II

04-005-020 Given an example of evidence for the theory of evolution and an interpretation of that evidence, determine whether this interpretation supports Darwin's theory of natural selection or Lamarck's theory of inheritance of acquired characteristics. IV

Describe and give examples of the following characteristics of the evolutionary process that produce changes within a species: stability factor, change factor, guiding factor, random genetic drift factor. II

Given a description of the evolution of a new species, recognize the mechanism of isolation that brought it about (e.g., isolation by time, geographic isolation, ecological isolation, and behavioral isolation). II

Discuss examples of genetic experiments involving polyploid chromosomes and the development of a new species. III

04-005-025 Describe the characteristics and functions of plant and animal cells. III

From a list that names cell structures or from a group of pictures or slides of living tissue that show cell structures, distinguish between cellular characteristics of plant and animal cells. III

Describe cell structures that are characteristic of both animal and plant cells. II

Explain the interrelationships among the following structures, basing your explanation on the degree of complexity of the structure: cell, tissue, organ, system, organism. II

Identify the materials that cells require to maintain life. I

Observe plant and animal cells under the microscope, describing the observable differences. II

Describe the following ways in which substances move through cell membranes: passive diffusion, active transport, ingestion. II

Identify the factors that affect the rate at which a solid solute goes into a liquid solvent. I

Suggest an experiment to test the permeability of various substances. II

Identify and list the functions of four structures of a plant cell (elodea) and three structures of an animal cell (cheek cell) as seen through a compound microscope. I

04-005-030 **Compare prokaryotic and eukaryotic cells on the basis of size and compartmentalization, and recognize examples of each type of cell. IV**

State why the eukaryotic cell is superior to the prokaryotic cell. I

Identify from a diagram, model, micrograph, or description the following nuclear structures of the cell: nucleus, nuclear envelope, chromosome (chromatin), nucleolus. I

Explain the functions of the following nuclear structures: nucleus, nuclear envelope, chromosome (chromatin), nucleolus. III

Identify from a diagram, model, micrograph, or description the following organelles located in the cytoplasm outside the nuclear envelope of a cell: plasma membrane (cell membrane), mitochondrion, endoplasmic reticulum (smooth and rough), Golgi bodies (Golgi apparatus), vacuole, and ribosome. I

Explain the functions of the following organelles located in the cytoplasm outside the nuclear envelope of a cell: plasma membrane (cell membrane), mitochondrion, endoplasmic reticulum, Golgi bodies (Golgi apparatus), vacuole, ribosome. III

Identify from a diagram, model, micrograph, or description those organelles found only in a plant or animal cell, and explain the functions of such organelles. III

Examine the ultrastructure of a chloroplast, and explain the functions of the grana, the stroma, and the DNA of the chloroplast. III

04-005-035 **Analyze the process of diffusion by diagram, description, or other means. IV**

Define the way in which cell membrane structure permits the diffusion of materials through the membrane in the special type of diffusion known as osmosis. I

Given a description of an experiment that demonstrates osmosis, compare the processes in the experiment with the processes that permit materials to enter and exit living cells. IV

Suggest how cell membrane, pore size, molecular size, and concentration of a substance may affect the tendency of the molecules of a substance to distribute themselves equally. II

Account for movement of molecules into a cell from an area of low concentration to one of high concentration by means of the process of active transport. II

Identify the cells, cell structures, cell substances, and cell conditions involved in stomatal operation. I

Indicate how the opening and closing of the stomata of a leaf facilitate the processes of photosynthesis and respiration in the leaf. I

Explain the effect on living cells of a change in pH level, and recognize how the pigment extracted from red cabbage leaves illustrates this effect. II

List four environmental factors that cause plants to exhibit tropisms or nastic responses, and prepare an experiment to illustrate a specific tropism in a plant. III

04-005-040 Discuss three reasons why man has devised and used schemes of classification since early recorded history. III

Identify the following individuals and their attempts to classify living organisms: Aristotle, Theophrastus, John Ray, Karl von Linne. I

Identify the proper sequence of categories from kingdom to species in the Linnaean system of classification. I

Explain why the category of organisms called Protista has recently been made a separate kingdom of biological classification. II

Identify the structural characteristics used to classify living organisms into these three kingdoms: Animalia, Plantae, Protista. I

List at least three reasons for the use of Latin as the language of classification. I

Classify the following organisms from phylum through species: man, dog, wolf, coyote. II

Recognize four ways in which plants vary and, by using a couplet key and specimens, diagrams, photographs, or slides, classify members of the following plant groups: bacteria, fungi, liverworts, mosses, Psilotum, horsetails, ferns, ginkgos, conifers, angiosperms. II

Construct a couplet key that classifies five given animate or inanimate objects. III

04-005-045 **Use a taxonomic key to classify three given animals and three given plants. Describe each step you used, and end with the scientific name of each animal.** III

Given a portion of a simple taxonomic chart, explain the relationships among the different branches. Starting anywhere on the chart, derive a description of an organism by working upward through the chart to the kingdom level. II

Given the class to which a vertebrate belongs, identify the kingdom, phylum, and class characteristics of that vertebrate. I

Describe the method by which plants are classified and scientifically named by accomplishing the following methods. II
1. Given several characteristics of a plant, recognize those used by taxonomists in classifying it.
2. Given the classification scheme for an organism, explain the binomial system of naming plants.

04-005-050 **Describe and draw structures of organisms that illustrate diversity among the lower animal phyla.** IV

Draw an amoeba and a paramecium, and label at least five structures for each organism. III

From a given photograph, projection slide, wet mount, or written set of characteristics, identify the protozoan class to which the organism belongs. I

List the basic life functions carried out by the higher animal groups that are not carried out by the Protozoa. I

List the characteristics of the coelenterates and recognize the following members: sea anemone, coral, Portuguese man-of-war, jellyfish. II

List two ways that flatworms differ from coelenterates, and recognize the characteristics of the three flatworm classes as represented by planarians, flukes, and tapeworms. II

Compare the *Ascaris* roundworm (phylum Aschelminthes) with the earthworm (phylum Annelida) on the basis of body cavity, body segmentation, and life-style, and recognize members of each phylum. IV

From a given written set of characteristics or from a specimen identify members of the following molluscan classes: bivalves (class Pelecypoda), snails and slugs (class Gastropoda), and squids and octopi (class Cephalopoda). I

Differentiate the insects, arachnids, and crustaceans on the basis of the number and type of the following structures: antennae, eyes, walking legs, wings, mouth parts, body parts. III

Identify at least ten external structures of the grasshopper, and explain the function of each of these structures. II

Recognize in which animal phylum the following characteristics first appear: multicellularity, blind gut or enteron, three germ layers, bilateral symmetry, complete gut, pseudocoelom, true coelom, segmentation. II

04-005-055 **Describe and illustrate examples of diversity among the higher animal phyla, and explain the significance of these differences. IV**

Differentiate between the protostomes and deuterostomes on at least two bases. IV

Present evidence that justifies the relationship of the phylum Echinodermata to the phylum Chordata. III

Identify phylum characteristics and representative members of the phylum Echinodermata. I

Diagram the water vascular system of the echinoderms, and explain its operation. III

Identify the characteristics of the phylum Chordata. I

Compare the lamprey and the shark on the following bases: skeleton, mouthparts, gill slits, appendages, outer covering   IV

Compare the fish, amphibian, and reptile on the bases of appendages, outer body covering, and gas exchange apparatus.   IV

Explain the significance of the "land egg," and relate it to the amnion and internal fertilization.   IV

Explain the relationship of the birds and mammals to the reptile.   II

04-005-060   Through diagrams, pictures, or models, demonstrate the adaptive powers of plants and animals.   III

Define *habitat.*   I

Match organisms with pictures, descriptions, or names of the habitats to which they are best adapted.   II

Match the breathing structure (lungs or gills) of a common animal to the habitat for which it is best suited.   II

Describe at least six animal structures and the ways they have aided the survival of particular animals.   II

Match descriptions or drawings of seeds with the means (including wind, water, or animals such as birds, mammals, and man) by which they travel from the parent plant to another plant.   II

Describe how two coloration patterns, protective coloration and advertisement, function for particular animals.   II

Identify some of the reasons why animals migrate.   I

Identify the methods and tools that man uses to track the migration routes of birds.   I

Identify correct statements of what happens within the animal's body during hibernation, and identify from a list those animals that hibernate.   I

Prepare and present a report on the following animal societies on the basis of the degree of organization of the members within the society: ants, bees, wasps, wolves, elephants, deer, termites. III

Explain the role of adaptation in evolution. II

04-005-065 **Describe adaptations of muscular and skeletal systems of three selected vertebrates and three selected invertebrates that aid each organism in obtaining food. II**

Identify the specific structural adaptations that enable organisms to acquire food. (Include frogs, jellyfish, snakes, protists, birds, and man.) I

Describe mouth adaptation with respect to the kinds of food to be gathered by an animal. II

Recognize how the skeletal and muscular systems of man and other common vertebrates are similar to those of arthropods (invertebrates) by classifying the support structures of each exoskeletal or endoskeletal system, and by recognizing the predominant types of muscular tissue in each system. II

Explain a schematic representation of how food consumed by man is used for growth and the production of energy and how waste products are eliminated through the coordinated action of the digestive, respiratory, circulatory, and excretory systems. II

04-005-070 **Using a specific plant and animal, develop an experiment that demonstrates the mechanism by which each obtains and produces energy and synthesizes organic compounds. V**

Explain the function of enzymes in aerobic and anaerobic systems. II

Given the name of organic compounds that serve as building blocks, identify the classes of compounds that the cell can synthesize from these building blocks. I

Given a description of the works of various scientists, explain how the work of each scientist is related to the total concept of photosynthesis. II

Given the generalized chemical reaction for photosynthesis, identify raw materials for the reaction, products of "light" and "dark" reactions, plant structures involved in the reactions, and environmental conditions necessary for the reactions.   I

Develop an experimental procedure to demonstrate factors in energy production.   V

04-005-075   Describe each of the structural components of vascular plants.   II

From a given specimen, model, or written description, identify the following twig structures and their functions: terminal and lateral buds, leaf and vascular bundle scars, node and internode, bud scale and bud-scale scar, lenticel.   I

Determine the age of a specific twig.   II

Recognize the following: simple, compound, and doubly compound leaves; parallel and netted venation; alternate, opposite, whorled leaf arrangement.   II

From a given drawing, model, microscope slide, or photograph, identify the following internal structures of a dicot leaf and recognize the function of each structure: cuticle, upper and lower epidermis, palisade layer, spongy layer, guard cell, stoma, xylem and phloem of a vein.   I

List the four main functions of a woody stem.   I

From a given drawing, model, microscope slide, or photograph, identify the following internal structures of a woody stem and recognize the function of each: wood fibers, tracheids, and vessels of xylem; sieve tubes, companion cells, and phloem fibers of phloem; cambium.   II

List the four main functions of a root.   I

Identify the four major regions of a root.   I

04-005-080   **Given a vascular plant and a nonvascular plant, describe the intake of nutrients and production of waste products, identifying the structures involved in each process. III**

Recognize the major structural parts, and explain the function served by each of these parts. II

Recognize the structural characteristics of roots that perform the functions of storage, absorption, and anchorage. II

Recognize the major structural parts of five samples of stems, and explain the functions served by these parts. II

Differentiate between the structural and functional characteristics of vascular and nonvascular plants. III

Describe the role of meristemic tissue and effects of chemicals (auxins, indoleacetic acid, 2,4-D) on the growth of plants. II

04-005-085   **Determine environmental factors affecting photosynthesis, and describe experiments that test whether light is necessary for photosynthesis, whether CO_2 is necessary for photosynthesis, and whether chlorophyll is necessary for photosynthesis. IV**

Diagram and interpret a curve that graphically illustrates the radiation reflection and/or absorption spectrum of any object provided. III

Explain the radiation spectrum in terms of a green leaf. II

Trace the transformation of energy from the sun to the ATP molecule. III

Identify the high-energy bonds that are formed in the ATP molecule, and interpret a diagram of the input and and outflow of energy in the ADP:ATP cycle. IV

Explain the events of the light reaction and the dark reaction of photosynthesis in terms of the raw materials and products of the photosynthetic process. II

Distinguish between anaerobic and aerobic respiration on the basis of materials needed, products, sites of activity, and energy yielded. IV

Compare photosynthesis with anaerobic and aerobic respiration in terms of the utilization or production of O_2, CO_2, sugar, water, and energy. IV

04-005-090 **Support the statement "Species survival is dependent upon efficient complementarity of structure and function." IV**

Explain the statement "In the world of life, there exists a complementarity of structure and function," and give one example to justify your explanation. III

Identify four gross plant structures, and relate these structures to their functions. II

Identify ten external and internal structures of the frog, and relate each of these structures to its function. II

Compare the flight mechanisms of a bird with those of a bat in terms of efficient structure–function relationships. IV

Compare energy relationships, eyesight, feeding habits, and body-temperature requirements of the bat and the bird, and hypothesize the special structures and functions the bat needs in order to compete with an insectivorous bird. IV

Given illustrations, models, or photographs, distinguish at least one example of structure-function complementarity for each organism or structure supplied. IV

04-005-095 **Develop a hypothesis that explains how multicellularity might bring about a higher behavioral level in multicellular forms. V**

Determine the ratio of surface area to volume in a one-inch cube and a two-inch cube, and explain your results in terms of multicellularity. IV

Explain the statement "Without multicellularity, organismal size is restricted." II

Define the terms *tissue, organ,* and *organ system,* and identify specific tissues, organs, or organ systems from given descriptions, diagrams, slides, or photographs. I

Identify the major types of tissues, and state a general function for each. I

Given a specific function, hypothesize the type of tissue that would best perform this function. IV

Compare an exoskeleton to an endoskeleton, and list at least two advantages for each. IV

Identify the following structures and types of cells, and explain their relationship to bone growth and repair: Haversian system (in compact bone), Haversian canal, lamellae, lacunae, epiphysis, diaphysis, epiphyseal plate, periosteum, compact bone, cancellous bone, osteolytic cells (osteoclasts), osteoblasts, osteocytes. II

Classify the three types of vertebrate muscle according to the type of cell structure they exhibit, their location in the body, and their special characteristics. II

Diagram or recognize a diagram of the sarcomere, the subcellular unit of the striated muscle, and explain its relationship to a muscle cell and to the entire muscle. II

Explain the contraction of a muscle by describing the hypothesized operation of an individual sarcomere. II

Given diagrams, models, or drawings of human-cell types, identify the tissue origin (blood, nerve, muscle, etc.) of the cell. I

04-005-100 **Compare and contrast the circulatory and respiratory systems in three types of higher animals. IV**

Recognize the relationship of gas exchange to the surface area and volume in a respiratory system. II

Identify three basic types of gas-exchange systems in animals, and recognize examples of animals in which these systems appear. II

Identify the following respiratory structures, and explain a function for each: nares, nasal cavity, glottis, larynx, trachea, bronchi, bronchioles, alveoli, lungs, diaphragm.   II

Compare a frog to a mammal on the basis of amount of lung surface area in relation to the size of the organism, and explain the amount of lung surface area in terms of each organism's life pattern.   IV

Explain the relationship of the surface area of alveoli to the surface area of capillaries.   II

Discuss the type of circulatory system found in specific organisms.   III

Compare the heart structure of fish, amphibians, reptiles, birds, and mammals.   IV

Identify two major changes that occur in the human infant's circulatory system at birth, and explain why these changes occur.   I

Trace the circulatory routes of blood in man.   III

04-005-105   Discuss the gathering, digestion, and utilization of food in animals, and evaluate the efficiency of specific animals in carrying out these processes.   VI

Distinguish between autotrophic and heterotrophic nutritional patterns, and formulate a hypothesis concerning the interdependency of the two.   VI

Compare the nutritional patterns of an herbivore, a carnivore, and an omnivore, and describe their dentition and digestive-tract anatomy.   IV

Compare the patterns of intracellular digestion with those of extracellular digestion within specific animal forms.   IV

Distinguish between mechanical and chemical digestion and the end products of each.   IV

Trace a particle of food through the human gastrointestinal tract, identify the mechanism for moving food along the tract, and explain how this mechanism works. III

Identify the major role of each of the following organs in the digestive system: mouth, esophagus, stomach, small intestine, colon. I

Identify the three major classes of molecules found in food and their intermediate and end products of digestion; then state a hypothesis that explains the action digestive enzymes have on these molecules. III

Construct and interpret a chart listing enzymes and other digestive "juices," their source of secretion, their site of action, their specific action, and the products of their activity. III

Explain the relationship of the absorption of digested foodstuffs to the surface area of the intestinal tract, and cite examples to illustrate this relationship. III

Recognize the following examples of non-energy-yielding substances that are essential to animal nutrition, and identify their function in the process of nutrition: vitamins (D, B_1, B_2, A) and minerals (calcium, iron, sodium, trace metals). II

04-005-110 **Describe the excretory system and explain the need for a proper tissue-fluid balance within an organism. III**

Recognize three functions of an excretory system and the role the lungs, skin, intestinal tract, and kidneys play in carrying out these functions. II

Explain the statement "At any specific point in time, the excretory system must determine what is a waste." II

Identify the three major nitrogenous waste products excreted by various animal groups. I

Recognize the advantages and disadvantages of excreting ammonia, urea, or uric acid, and identify which animal groups excrete which waste product. II

Identify and label on a diagram the anatomical structures of the kidney and the urinary ducts. I

Describe the function of the kidney by tracing the processes of filtration, reabsorption, and secretion in the nephron, and explain the relationship these processes have to the nephron's structure. II

Explain how the following substances are processed by the nephron, and determine whether they are actively or passively reabsorbed or secreted: glucose, sodium, amino acids, hydrogen ions, water, penicillin, and urea. III

Predict how specific physiological conditions affect the volume of urine produced by the kidneys. III

04-005-115 **Describe the operation of the components of a homeostatic system, and analyze the importance of homeostasis. IV**

Discuss the contributions that Hippocrates, Claude Bernard, and Walter Cannon made to the concept of homeostasis. I

Explain the concept of homeostasis in terms of the thermostatic control of room temperature. II

Identify the events that occur to regulate the control of fluids in the circulatory system of a mammal. I

Name the events that occur to regulate the intake of fluids in a mammal. I

04-005-120 **Analyze the manner in which hormones function as regulatory substances within the endocrine systems of vertebrates. IV**

Recognize five historical developments that contributed to our knowledge of the endocrine system. II

Identify and order the classical techniques used to determine whether a specific sample of glandular tissue produces a hormone. I

Match the following glands with their location in the body, the hormones they secrete, and the activity regulated by the hormones: adrenal cortex, adrenal medulla, thyroid, parathyroid, pancreas, neurohypophysis. I

Identity the six hormones secreted by the adenohypophysis, the anterior lobe of the pituitary gland; determine whether these hormones are trophic, and identify the activities they regulate. IV

Explain the cause of *diabetes mellitus* in terms of its major symptoms, and explain how the injection of insulin reduces these symptoms. II

Match the following disease conditions with a given set of symptoms and a given endocrine gland malfunction: acromegaly, cretinism, giantism, goiter, midget, exophthalmic goiter. I

04-005-125 Discuss the relationship among the parts of the human nervous system. IV

List the three principal components of a stimulus-response reaction, and recognize the modifications of these components as found in advanced organisms. II

Recognize the neuron as the basic cellular unit of a communication or coordinating system, and recognize the meaning of the following terms associated with neurons: *dendrites, axon, cell body, Schwann cells, myelin sheath, motor neuron, sensory neuron, association neuron, synapse.* II

Trace the pathway of the reflex arc in a person who has just stepped on a sharp object. II

Recognize the anatomical structure of the human brain and the function of each of its parts. II

Recognize the anatomical structure of the spinal cord and the function of each of its parts, and explain the function of the spinal cord in the reflex arc. II

Recognize the relationship of the central nervous system to the autonomic nervous system and its two sub-divisions, the sympathetic and the parasympathetic systems.   II

Recognize the nature of the nerve impulse and the following terms associated with nerve transmission: *sodium, potassium, sodium–potassium pump, depolarization, repolarization.*   II

04-005-130   Perceive the relationship of the behavior of a person who is threatened and then struck by an object and the resultant behavioral changes in the endocrine and nervous systems. Emphasize the interrelatedness of the activities of these systems.   IV

Given the major structures of the endocrine system, identify each of the following.   I
1. The major functions of each structure
2. The method of hormone transfer
3. The major function of the entire endocrine system

Given the major structures of the nervous system of man, do each of the following.   II
1. Classify each structure as a part of the central, autonomic, or peripheral nervous system.
2. Describe nerve cells as motor (efferent), sensory (afferent), or associative (connective) nerve cells.
3. Identify axons, dendrites, cell body, neurilemma, and myelin on a neuron.
4. Describe the general functions of the medulla, cerebrum, and cerebellum.
5. Recognize examples of endocrine or nervous-system activities that regulate internal bodily functions (i.e., heartbeat, body temperature, pupil dilation, blood-vessel construction, and enzyme secretion).

04-005-135   Through research, investigate the process by which DNA was discovered and its molecular structure determined.   III

Recognize the structure and components of a DNA molecule.   II

Match the bases in a DNA molecule, and match a single strand of DNA with its complementary strand.   I

Describe the steps in DNA replication, and explain the nuclear changes that occur in the phases of mitosis.   II

Recognize the mitotic phase in which DNA replication occurs.   II

Describe the cytokinetic events in plant cells and in animal cells during telophase that lead to new cell formation.   II

Identify the phases indicated in a given photograph of mitotic cells.   I

Discuss the role of mitosis in the growth of a human adult from a fertilized egg cell.   III

04-005-140   Discuss the characteristics of seeds and the conditions required for plant growth.   III

Identify the following structures in a monocot seed and state a function for each structure: pericarp, endosperm, cotyledon, embryo, coleoptile, plumule, radicle, coleorhiza.   I

Identify the following structures in a dicot seed, and state a function for each structure: seed coat, cotyledons, embryo, epicotyl, radicle, hypocotyl.   I

Describe the development of a bean seed into a young plant.   II

Explain the concept of seed dormancy, and list at least three factors that affect dormancy.   II

List three conditions necessary for the germination of a seed.   I

Recognize the three phases of growth of a plant, and identify these stages on a growth curve.   II

Explain the relationships between temperature and plant growth and between light and plant growth.   II

Identify the four regions of meristematic tissue in a plant, and state a function for each region. I

04-005-145   Discuss the systems of the human body—digestive, circulatory, respiratory, nervous, reproductive, glandular, excretory, skeletal, muscular, and integumentary—with respect to the important general functions of each system. III

Describe the function of the human skeleton, and locate on a diagram the major bone structures: skull, rib cage, backbone, pelvis, femur, tibia, fibula, radius, ulna, phalanges. II

Identify the locations and functions of the major parts of the central nervous system: the brain (cerebellum, cerebrum, and medulla), and the spinal cord. I

Draw a diagram of the digestive system, and label the parts and identify the function of each: salivary glands, mouth, general esophagus, sphincter muscles, stomach, gall bladder, liver, pancreas, large intestine, small intestine, appendix, rectum. III

Define *enzyme,* and identify the specific function of each of the following digestive enzymes: amylase, pepsin, trypsin, chymotrypsin, peptidase, dipeptidase, maltase, sucrase, lactase, lipase. I

Discuss the function of the parts of the human circulatory system, including the following: heart, capillary, artery, vein, arteriole. III

Identify the major constituent differences between whole blood and blood plasma, the major functions of each in the body, and the purpose they serve in transfusions. I

Explain the differences between blood and lymph, including their parts and major functions in the human body. II

Describe the normal flow of air in and out of the human respiratory system. II

Given a diagram of the respiratory system, label the following parts and identify the function of each: epiglottis, larynx, trachea, lung, bronchus, air sacs, diaphragm. I

Identify the location of the following endocrine glands in the human body, and identify the secretion(s) produced by each gland and the body function that each secretion controls: pituitary, thyroid, parathyroid, pancreas, adrenal cortex, adrenal medulla, male reproductive organs, female reproductive organs. I

Given a diagram of the excretory system for liquid waste, label the following parts and identify the function of each part: post-caval vein, renal artery, kidney, renal vein, ureter, blood vessels to leg, bladder. I

02-005-150 **Define the term disease and relate it to microorganisms. IV**

Recognize characteristics of the virus–host relationship, and explain why it is described as a master–slave relationship. II

Identify characteristics of bacteria in terms of size relative to other organisms, basic shapes, and motility. I

Recognize the relationship of asexual reproduction of bacteria to the growth curve of a bacterial population and the incubation period of an infectious disease. II

Determine whether the following diseases are caused by bacteria or by viruses: pneumonia, influenza, common cold, tuberculosis, measles, smallpox, syphilis, typhoid fever, diphtheria. III

Define the term *virulence,* and list five factors that affect it. I

Distinguish between endotoxins and exotoxins, and compare their relative toxicity to man. IV

Explain the difference between active immunity and passive immunity. II

Identify at least four means of controlling the active growth of bacteria. II

List at least five ways in which bacteria are beneficial to man. I

04-005-155   Investigate the characteristics of given organisms that are harmful to man, and explain means of controlling these organisms. III

Explain the structures and functions of four general groups of disease-causing microorganisms: virus, fungus, bacteria, protozoa. II

Correctly label given drawings or descriptions of each of the three types of bacteria: coccus, bacillus, spirillum. I

Given examples of common household or professional medical practices, tell whether chemicals, heat, or antibiotics are being used to combat infectious bacteria. I

Given a list of scientists who have studied microorganisms (Louis Pasteur, Edward Jenner, Joseph Lister, Jonas Salk, Alexander Fleming, Robert Koch) and their scientific discoveries, match the scientist with his discovery. I

Explain the differences in the following types of diseases: organic, allergic, infectious, deficiency. II

Given a description of a particular disease and the way it is contracted, classify the disease as communicable or noncommunicable. II

Explain the ways in which specific disease-causing organisms enter the body: entry with water, milk, or food; entry with the air; and entry through the skin. List one means of preventing each of these problems. II

Explain the body's lines of defense that help in resisting and/or combating disease-causing microorganisms. II

Identify the most effective methods used to prevent the spread of disease. I

04-005-160   On the basis of your knowledge of the effect of environmental factors on the growth of microorganisms, discuss factors that make a microorganism infectious or noninfectious to a particular host.   III

Identify the similarities between the ecology of soil microorganisms and the ecology of larger animals.   I

Describe the ecological relationships between microorganisms and multicellular plants in the nitrogen cycle.   II

Discuss ways in which the human body protects itself against pathogenic microorganisms.   III

Reasonably predict the fate of a mammalian embryo and the embryo of one other animal if mechanisms for protection and nourishment should break down during the vulnerable embryonic and preembryonic period of their development.   III

Given a description of a disease, classify the disease as infectious or noninfectious. If it is infectious, identify the vector, the pathogen, the host, and the method of disease transmission.   II

Explain how the processes expressed in Koch's postulates relate to developments in the science of epidemiology.   II

04-005-165   Collect information about and discuss four types of human diseases.   III

Summarize six articles from magazines or newspapers about research that scientists are doing on at least one disease, and present an oral or a written report on your findings.   III

Identify the ways in which each of the following are harmful to humans: rickettsiae, fungi, bacteria, viruses, protozoa, algae.   I

Identify the ways in which each of the following organisms are helpful to humans: fungi, viruses, protozoa, algae, bacteria.   I

Define each of the following, and identify examples of each when described: *symbiosis, parasitism, mutualism, commensalism.*   I

Prepare and present a report tracing the research history of diabetes and insulin; include recent information on diabetes reported by medical research and a description of the contributions that each of the following scientists made to the discovery and use of insulin: Von Mering, Minkowski, Banting, MacCleod, Best.   III

Prepare and present an oral report, or prepare diagrams and pictures, about a disease in which you are interested, and trace the research done by scientists on this disease throughout the last fifty years.   III

Identify the type of organism (bacterium, virus, or protozoan) that causes each of the following diseases, and describe the method(s) of transmission and prevention for each disease.   II

1. Tuberculosis	12. Meningitis
2. Diphtheria	13. Whooping cough
3. Typhoid	14. Dysentery
4. Colds	15. Cholera
5. Influenza	16. Tetanus
6. Measles	17. Gas gangrene
7. Chicken pox	18. Botulism
8. Smallpox	19. Anthrax
9. Mumps	20. Rabies
10. Poliomyelitis	21. Tularemia
11. Psittacosis	

04-005-170   **Compare reasons that people who drink alcoholic beverages give to justify their actions with reasons given by drug users to justify their use of drugs.   IV**

Collect information about and discuss the effects of tobacco, alcohol, and drugs on the human body, using reliable reports of research.   III

From a given description of symptoms, recognize symptoms that describe the physiological effects of smoking on the human body.   II

Describe three ways to help a smoker stop his habit.   II

From a given description of symptoms, recognize symptoms that describe the physiological effects of alcohol on the human body.   II

On a diagram, trace the path alcohol takes as it is absorbed into the bloodstream, and identify three principal parts of the body that are adversely affected.   II

Identify three steps that a moderate drinker can take to prevent himself from becoming an alcoholic.   I

From a given description of symptoms, recognize symptoms that describe the psychological effects of specific drugs on the human body.   II

Identify proper and improper uses of amphetamines and depressants.   I

Describe at least one possible immediate physiological effect and one possible aftereffect on human beings who use marijuana.   II

Suggest ways in which the improper use of drugs might be avoided.   II

Discuss steps that have been taken to rehabilitate alcoholics or drug addicts.   III

04-005-175   **Discuss the human reproductive system and describe present-day mores related to reproduction.   III**

Describe the similarities in the reproductive systems in animals and in flowering plants.   II

Explain the reasons for the bodily changes that occur in males and females during puberty.   II

Describe the functions of the reproductive organs in the human male and the human female.   II

Recognize correct definitions of each of the following terms, and explain the relationship of each to the total development of a mammal: *gametes, coitus, fertilization, zygote, blastula, gastrula, fetus, birth.*   II

Discuss population growth in relation to economic climate.   III

Support or refute suggestions for altering the reproductive patterns of people.   III

04-005-180   Compare and contrast the reproductive process in plants, insects, and animals.   IV

Identify the fruit and the four main parts (roots, stems, leaves, flowers) of a flowering plant, and explain the basic function of the main parts.   II

Define each of the following: fission, budding, spore formation, regeneration, vegetative reproduction. Recognize drawings or descriptions of each.   I

Recognize the body parts of a mealworm—antenna, head, mouth, leg, thorax, abdomen—and describe their functions.   II

Identify the body parts of an insect you choose to study.   II

Define each of the following stages: *adult, larva, egg, pupa.* Identify examples of these stages in the metamorphosis of a butterfly, a fly, and a mosquito.   I

Recognize the difference between complete and incomplete metamorphosis.   II

Keep a record of your observations of the developmental stages.   III

Describe the conditions of birth, the appearance of the newborn, and the life requirements of the newborn of each of the following animals: man, dog, chicken, turtle, fish, frog.   II

04-005-185 Use specific examples drawn from the plant and animal kingdom to show your understanding of ways the differences in the mechanisms of mitosis and meiosis affect the offspring that result from asexual or sexual reproduction. III

Given diagrams of various stages of mitosis, identify in which phase the cell exists. I

Identify the following asexual methods of reproduction: budding, fission, spore formation, vegetative reproduction. Include definitions, examples, and comparisons. I

Explain the difference between asexual reproduction and sexual reproduction by describing the general processes involved in each type as well as the genetic advantages and disadvantages that are characteristic of each type of reproduction. II

Identify the general sequence by which the monoploid (haploid) gametes are developed during the process of meiosis. I

Recognize the parts of the reproductive structure of mosses, ferns, and flowering plants. Describe the function of each structure, considering reproductive parts of each type of plant, plant structure in which meiosis occurs, and sequence of the alternation of generations for each. II

Define the following terms as they are related to reproduction: *gamete formation, self-fertilization, hermaphroditism, unisexual, parthenogenesis.* I

04-005-190 Compare and contrast the appearance of fish, bird, and pig embryos at comparable stages of development, and indicate the significance of the similarities and differences. IV

Define the process of cleavage, and identify the resulting stages. I

Identify and describe the different stages of cleavage, blastulation, and gastrulation; identify the structures formed in each stage, and explain what happens to these structures in the embryo. II

Match the three embryonic germ layers with the tissues and organs that arise from each of them.   I

Compare the embryonic development of a hydra, an earthworm, a fish, a frog, a bird, and a mammal, according to the following characteristics.   IV
1. Development within the body of the mother or external to the mother
2. Presence of yolk sac or placenta
3. Method by which nourishment is supplied to the embryo
4. Method by which the embryo is protected
5. Method by which oxygen is supplied to the embryo

Trace the development of the embryo in mammals, and include a description of the formation of eggs and sperm, the sex organs involved in transporting the egg and sperm, the union of egg and sperm, the sequence of development from zygote through embryo and fetus to birth, and hormonal changes.   III

Explain how Hans Spemann and Hilde Mangold's experiments support the principle of induction.   II

Recognize two stressful environmental changes to which the newly born organism is subjected, and explain the nature of these stresses.   II

Explain the differences in appearance and behavior of a newly hatched robin and a newly hatched chick, and formulate a principle to explain these differences; define the terms *precocial* and *altricial*.   IV

04-005-195   Compare the processes of mitosis and meiosis on the following bases: desired outcome in terms of chromosome number, number of cells produced, fate of cells produced, site of occurrence in man.   IV

Explain the necessity for a reduction in chromosome number in the sex cells.   II

Trace chromosome behavior in meiosis, and compare it to chromosome behavior in mitosis.   IV

Diagram the chromosome pattern in each of the following stages of meiosis: prophase I, metaphase I, anaphase I, prophase II, metaphase II, anaphase II, late telophase. III

Recognize the phase of meiosis during which reduction division occurs. II

04-005-200 **Given the genotype of an individual, determine all the possible gene combinations in the gametes that can be formed by that plant or animal. IV**

Determine hypothetical ratios from Mendel's experimental data. IV

Define the following genetic terms and support your definition with genetic data: *dominant* and *recessive, phenotype* and *genotype, homozygous* and *heterozygous,* F_1 and F_2. III

Interpret Mendel's law of segregation, and give an example to support your interpretation. III

Interpret Mendel's law of independent assortment, and give an example to support your interpretation. III

Account for the inheritance pattern called incomplete dominance. II

Complete the Punnett squares for the F_2 generations of monohybrid and dihybrid genetic crosses. II

04-005-205 **Combine concepts, principles, and generalizations by designing an experiment with fruit flies to illustrate Mendel's laws. Complete each stage of the experiment, and evaluate your results. V**

Given an example of evidence for the theory of evolution and interpretation of that evidence, conclude whether this interpretation supports Darwin's theory of natural selection or Lamarck's theory of inheritance of acquired characteristics. II

Discuss the factors characteristic of the evolutionary process that produce changes within a species: stability, change, guiding (fertility and viability), random genetic drift factor.   III

Discuss the factors in the evolution of a new species, emphasizing the type of isolation that brought the evolution about (i.e., isolation by time, geographic isolation, ecological isolation, and behavioral isolation).   III

Given a description of Mendel's experiments, recognize examples of the following.   II
1. Dominant traits and recessive traits
2. Pure breeding and hybridization
3. P_1, F_1, F_2, F_3 . . . generation
4. Homozygous or heterozygous genotypes

Given the genotype of the parents and a list of the possible genotype and phenotype combinations, predict the probable ratios of the genotypes and phenotypes of the offspring.   III

Given an example of dihybrid cross, apply the principles of segregation and independent assortment by stating the behavior of the alleles involved.   III

Identify the major ideas in the chromosome theory.   I

Recognize examples of how scientists have applied genetic experiments involving polyploid chromosomes to the development of a new species.   II

Explain the gene theory of mutations by differentiating between gene mutation and chromosomal mutation, by describing the biochemical nature of genes (include the general structure and composition of DNA and how the internal arrangement affects the variations), and by identifying abiotic conditions that have been observed to affect the biochemistry of the genes.   II

04-005-210   Discuss examples of sex-limited inheritance.   III

Indicate the sex chromosome pattern in the human male and female.   I

Identify traits that are sex-linked, and solve problems involving red-green color blindness and hemophilia in males. I

Identify causes and symptoms of phenylketonuria, alcaptonuria and albinism. I

Recognize examples of and define the term *nondisjunction.* II

Identify symptoms of and recognize the inheritance mechanisms for Turner's and Klinefelter's syndromes. I

Identify symptoms of and recognize the inheritance mechanism for Down's syndrome. I

Indicate how Barr bodies can be used in the determination of sex. I

04-005-215 **Draw and analyze your family tree or the family tree of an acquaintance. Attempt to explain the presence of three family traits according to Mendel's laws and according to present-day knowledge of genetics, citing the scientist responsible for theories you use. IV**

Define and identify examples of the following genetic terms: *sex-linked traits, crossing over, nonallelic genes, nondominance, nondisjunction, linkage, multiple alleles, mutations, chromosome mapping.* I

Explain the gene theory of mutations by using the following procedures. II
1. Distinguish between gene mutation and chromosomal mutation.
2. Describe the biochemical nature of genes (include the general structure and composition of DNA and how the internal arrangement affects the variations).
3. Identify abiotic conditions that have been observed to affect the biochemistry of genes.

Identify human traits, such as color blindness, that are believed to be associated with one or more of the following: sex-linked genes, nondominance, nondisjunction, multiple alleles. I

Match the following scientists with their contributions to genetics: Gregor Mendel, Walter Sutton, Calvin S. Bridges, Thomas Morgan, H. J. Muller, James D. Watson and Francis H. Crick, George Beadle and Edward Tatum, and Karl Correns, Hugo de Vries, and Erich Tschermak. I

04-005-220 Compare innate behavior to learned behavior. IV

Define *behavior,* and suggest three purposes of behavior. II

Define and give examples of tropisms, suggest their adaptive significance, and describe a type of plant movement that is not a tropism. II

Identify these types of innate behavior and indicate their adaptive significance: taxis, reflex, and instinct. II

Describe the function of courtship patterns and territoriality. II

Define *dominance hierarchy,* and suggest the function of the pecking order in chickens. II

Explain how dominance hierarchy in a baboon troop differs from pecking order in chickens, and suggest the adaptive value of baboon social structure. II

Identify types of learned behavior, and give examples of each. I

Indicate levels of learned behavior possible in different levels of organisms. II

Draw conclusions about the effects of social deprivation on baby monkeys. IV

04-005-225 Use correct terminology to describe learned and unlearned behavior in a group of selected animals observed for several hours. III

Describe the following behaviors: irritability, tropism, traces (taxis), positive and negative reactions to stimuli. II

Suggest examples of innate behavior (reflexes and instincts), learned behavior (conditioning, trial-and-error), and reasoning in animals. II

Given a discription of one of the following types of behaviors in vertebrates, recognize whether the behavior is learned or unlearned. II
1. Food-getting behavior
2. Escape and/or protective behavior
3. Reproductive behavior
4. Social behavior
5. Locational behavior (territorial and home range, homing, and migration)

Discuss activities that illustrate social behavior among such insects as honeybees, ants, and termites. III

Perform an experiment, using small animals, to test a hypothesis related to learned behavior. III

04-005-230 **Combine concepts, principles, and generalizations by designing an experiment in which the following principles of learning are demonstrated: learned and unlearned behavior, memorization, forgetting, and relearning. Include these procedures in the experiments. V**
1. **Formulate a hypothesis based on observations.**
2. **Organize your experiment with variables.**
3. **Draw conclusions and make generalizations.**
4. **Write a formal report of your findings.**

Differentiate between a stimulus and a response in a given situation. IV

In a given experiment that involves stimulus and response in living things, determine which variables are controlled (kept the same) and which ones are changed. IV

Given a list of ordinary, everyday acts performed by animals and human beings, recognize the difference between actions that are learned and actions that are not learned (reflex). II

From several groups of words or numbers, determine the group that is probably most easily memorized. Explain the reason why the group selected is the easiest to remember.   IV

Given a list of things present in a place of study, explain the difference between those that will not prevent learning and those that will.   II

Given an experiment on practice and memorization, recognize the variables that were controlled, and explain the ways in which they were controlled.   II

Explain which variables were controlled in an experiment on forgetting and relearning.   II

Given a simple graph on which a series of test scores has been plotted, explain the reasons the scores changed from test to test.   II

Given different forms of graphs showing test scores, explain which forms can be compared most easily and interpret the scores.   II

04-005-235   **Trace the flow of energy from the sun, through the living system, and back into the abiotic environment.   III**

Given lists of chemical elements, identify those chemical elements commonly found in living organisms.   I

Give evidence to show that matter (water, CO_2, N_2, and calcium) moves cyclically between the nonliving world and the living world—the biosphere.   I

Using information concerning biotic (living environmental) and abiotic (physical environmental) factors, identify the effects that these would have on a given population.   I

04-005-240   **Construct and analyze a food web based on a given chart of a biomass pyramid.   IV**

Define the terms *species, population, community,* and *ecosystem.*   I

Explain the relationship of carbon and nitrogen cycles to a generalized food web. II

Recognize the effect that soil, sun, water, pH, and ionic concentration have on an ecosystem. II

Discuss ways in which organisms solve the problem of competition by being adapted to a niche or habitat or by using spacing or social hierarchy. III

04-005-245 **Relate marine biotic forms to their abiotic environment by describing environmental conditions found in the spray, intertidal, and subtidal zones, and give examples of the types of marine organisms that could best survive in each zone. IV**

Given a description of a biotic interrelationship that exists in a specific ecological community, state whether the relationship is an example of commensalism, mutualism, competition, scavenging, parasitism, or predation. I

Define and recognize examples of community succession. II

Given a description of changes in an abiotic variable (temperature and relative humidity) common to several communities, explain how these abiotic changes can affect members in the biotic communities. II

Identify patterns and interrelationships that exist between producers and consumers in a pond community. I

Explain the roles of living organisms that act as food producers and those that act as first-, second-, or third-order food consumers. II

Describe the abiotic factors of headwaters, lakes, deltas, and lower and middle reaches of streams, and name the organisms that best survive in those areas. I

Describe the environmental conditions that are the major determiners of the types of organisms that can survive in particular environments. II

Using biome maps and climatogram information, identify the major abiotic environmental factors that determine a specific biome type. II

Discuss the general biotic conditions that are common to most biomes. III

04-005-250 Analyze four processes that are related to most patterns of ecological succession. IV

Compare the growth patterns of a city and those of a forest. IV

Hypothesize the environmental conditions that are necessary for the growth of cottonwood trees. IV

Recognize the sequential nature of succession, and identify three stages in sand-dune succession. II

Trace the various stages of a pond succession. II

Describe the effect of a disturbance on the process of succession. IV

04-005-255 Analyze a problem related to pollution, and suggest a solution. IV

Explain natural pollution in terms of animal life cycles. II

Discuss succession, eutrophication, and environmental pollution with respect to changes in a lake. III

Recognize the synergistic effect of some environmental pollutants. II

Explain the term *biodegradable,* and discuss the reasons why it has become an issue in regard to present-day waste products. III

Analyze different methods of solid waste, sewage, and liquid waste disposal. IV

Identify variables that affect the rate of decomposition of organic materials, and describe the processes involved. II

04-005-260 **Draw conclusions about the effect that man's ability to control his environment has on other living things. Include at least three examples of control and the means used to apply it. IV**

Identify the major physiological and behavioral characteristics that distinguish man from other primates. I

Recognize examples of mutualism that contribute to, or are found in, the human culture. Consider products of domestication and cultivation. II

Predict which of several experiments is best designed to answer a given question about the effect of such variables as temperature, air supply, light, water, and food on behavior or growth of an organism in its environment. III

Review information from any sources that demonstrate the absence of an organism necessary to maintain a balance of interrelation between plants and animals in a particular area. Suggest a plan for correcting the imbalance in the environment. II

Identify and analyze the methods that humans have used or could use to transform a specific biome, making it more adaptable to their way of life. IV

04-005-265 **Given the continuation of the expansion of cities and the destruction of natural life, predict the changes that may occur in the total environment. Report evidence to support your predictions. III**

Support the following hypothesis by experimental procedures: "If one of the reactants (variables) is removed from the photosynthetic reaction in green plants, then these plants cannot produce food." III

Recognize a drawing of the carbon cycle, and describe the functional interrelationships among the parts of the cycle. II

Recognize a drawing of the nitrogen cycle, and describe the functional interrelationships among the parts of the cycle. II

Explain the difference between a food chain and a food web, and describe the interrelationships of food chains in a food web with respect to the human population.   II

Define the terms *predator, parasite,* and *scavenger,* and identify examples of each.   I

Explain the effects that the removal of one part of a food web would have on the total environment of a given habitat.   II

Given an example of a food chain, trace the flow of energy through the chain and relate the following terms to the type of organism involved: *producer, consumer, saprophyte, predator.*   II

Given a description of characteristics of a plant or plant products, explain how the plant products are useful or beneficial to man.   II

Predict the response of a particular plant to specific growing conditions, apply the conditions in an experiment, and write a laboratory report on the result.   III

Given information on the interrelationship of living things in a pond, describe the benefits of one plant or animal to the other plants and animals.   II

Identify the main forces that erode the soil, and tell how each force contributes to the erosion.   I

Define the term *conservation,* and identify ways of preventing soil erosion.   I

Match listed causes of air pollution to related forms of prevention.   I

Match listed causes of water pollution to related forms of prevention.   I

Prepare a demonstration of soil erosion, and record the changes in the original topology of your example as you alter the forces on the soil.   III

04-005-270 **Compare human and animal population growth curves. IV**

Demonstrate your ability to perceive the effect of uncontrolled population growth by conducting an experiment involving small fish, such as guppies; report your observations graphically, analyze your results, and speculate on the significance of this experiment in regard to uncontrolled human population growth. IV

Identify characteristics that describe individuals and those that describe populations. I

Demonstrate changes in population densities by defining *population density,* identifying the major population determiners that increase and those that decrease population density, and using the density formula to calculate the numerical change in a population when the effects of a specified population determiner are given. III

Using information concerning biotic (living environmental) and abiotic (physical environmental) factors, predict the effects that these factors would have on a given population. III

Given graphs or descriptions of population changes, recognize changes that show the growth of a new population, the irregular population fluctuation, and a population cycle. II

Recognize the effects of human overpopulation on air, water, food supply, living space, noise level, and natural resources. II

Predict the effects of overcrowding on human behavior. II

Identify animal population controls in nature. I

Recognize current efforts to solve the popullution problem. II

04-005-275   **Given a scientific question or problem involving biology, combine concepts, principles, and generalizations by developing relevant hypotheses that can be tested through a series of experiments.   V**

Given a scientific event or situation, suggest questions that help to explain the event or situation.   II

Given a question, the answer to which would help explain a scientific event or situation, suggest sources of information or activities that may lead to an answer to the question.   II

Given a possible answer to a scientific question, develop a hypothesis that can be tested that may provide an answer to the question.   V

Develop a hypothesis based on observations and inferences drawn from biological science. (A hypothesis is an idea stated in such a way that it can be tested.)   V

Given a description of a biological experiment, recognize the following stages in its development: discovery of the problem, gathering information, formation of a testable hypothesis, performance of an experiment to test the hypothesis, and interpretation of the results and formation of conclusions.   II

04-005-280   **Analyze statistics, tables, and charts, and use the information to interpret biological data.   IV**

Record biological data in a table and a graph.   III

Convert scientific data contained in a graph into a table.   II

Interpret the way two biological variables are related, as shown in a graph.   II

04-005-285   **Discuss the total magnification of any combination of objective and eyepiece powers on a microscope with respect to specimens to be studied.   III**

Recognize the basic function of a compound microscope, and identify its potential uses and limitations.   II

Identify the parts of a microscope, and state a function for each part. I

Recognize rules for the use and care of the microscope, and state a reason for each rule. II

Demonstrate the steps involved in bringing a specimen into view on the microscope, using the low-power objective and using the high-power objective; predict the observable changes in position when a specimen is placed on and moved about the stage of a microscope; and locate and identify given specimens or objects in the microscope field. III

Prepare wet-mount slides for use with the microscope. III

04-005-290 **Combine concepts, principles, and generalizations by designing an investigation of a biological problem that involves the use of the microscope and other tools of the modern biologist. V**

Identify a correct statement of the function served by such instruments as the microscope and the thermometer in scientific observation. I

Given descriptions of particular attitudes or beliefs, describe those formed after scientific observation and those based upon previously formed or untested beliefs. II

Given a scientific event or situation, suggest questions that would help to explain the event or situation, and suggest sources of information or activities that may lead to an answer to the question. II

Given a hypothesis that can be tested, design a laboratory procedure or experiment that will test the hypothesis. III

After observing objects and events in the field of biology and using each of your five senses as appropriate, record the observations in terms of amounts whenever possible. II

Given a statement of observations from an experiment, classify each as a qualitative observation or a quantitative observation. II

Given a description of the work of nineteenth-century scientists, such as Louis Pasteur and Robert Koch, identify the phases of their work that would not have been possible without Leeuwenhoek's development of the microscope. III

04-005-295 Demonstrate your familiarity with medical terminology related to the body systems, including disorders. III

On a diagram identify parts of the body system and locate areas of disorders. I

Show that you can pronounce and spell medical terms and that you can understand medical reports. II

Take notes in outline form from printed medical reports and from oral reports. III

Using a medical dictionary, write a paragraph explaining a medical report to the layman. III

Earth Science

04-010-005 **Show that you can determine locations of areas represented on maps and use topographic information accurately. IV**

Estimate, to the nearest minute, the latitude and longitude of a point on a map. III

Read the magnetic declination from information provided on a map, and correct a compass to compensate for this error. II

Convert any one of the following map scales into another: graphic scale, representative fraction, verbal scale, projection. III

Identify topographic map symbols. I

Locate, to the nearest quarter of a quarter-section, a point on the land-grid system in areas of the country that have this system. II

Using contour lines, find the elevation of five points on a topographic map. II

Explain the use of colors on USGS topographic maps. II

Given the contours of two hill slopes, describe which slope is steeper. II

Construct a profile view along a line drawn between two points on a topographic map. III

Given a profile and appropriate scale data, calculate vertical exaggeration. II

04-010-010 **Discuss the relative positions of the various astronomical bodies in the universe. Describe the nature of forces among the astronomical bodies. III**

Identify the relative positions of the following astronomical bodies in the universe: stars, planets, our solar system, our galaxy, asteroids, meteoroids, comets. I

Draw a diagram that represents the order of the planets from the sun, and be able to discuss the relative distances of the planets. III

Given a description of movements in space or the gravitational attraction between two bodies, use the formula for gravity $F_g = (GM_1 \times M_2)/d^2$ as a basis for formulating a general mathematical interpretation. III

Explain how knowledge of gravitational force was used to predict the presence of Neptune and Pluto before they were discovered and the presence of large quantities of light gases on the major planets. II

04-010-015 Describe the planet Earth in relation to the solar system, and discuss ways in which it is typical or atypical. III

Define the term *solar system*. I

Describe the following physical characteristics of the sun: size, temperature, internal area or core, photosphere, chromosphere, corona, prominences, sunspots. II

Explain how the sun produces energy, and describe the sequence ot events that will take place in the sun's evolution as it begins to run out of hydrogen fuel. II

For each of the planets of the solar system, describe the type of atmosphere, number of moons or satellites, size relative to Earth, and major physical features. II

Explain the probable origin of the asteroid belt. II

Describe a comet's physical features and orbit. II

Compute the orbital velocity of a planet in kilometers per hour. III

04-010-020 Present the problems related to space travel, based on information gained from manned and unmanned spaceflights. III

Diagram and describe the rotation and revolution of the moon, and show why the same side of the moon's surface faces Earth at all times. III

Diagram the phases of the moon, showing the relative positions of Earth, the sun, and the moon at new, crescent, quarter, gibbous, and full stages. III

Explain and diagram the following types of eclipses: total solar, annular solar, partial solar, partial lunar, total lunar. III

Describe and locate on a lunar globe or lunar map each of the following features: maria (seas), craters, mountains, rills, rays. II

Discuss methods of lunar exploration from Galileo to the Apollo spaceflights, and relate the results to the study of the branches of earth science. III

Interpret, with respect to space travel, some of the findings gathered on recent unmanned spaceflights to Mars, including two findings that indicate the probable presence of an atmosphere. II

Outline the probable developments in space travel for the near future and their benefits to humans. II

04-010-025 Determine the relationship of our galaxy to other galaxies. IV

Describe the variables that influence the brightness and color of a star. II

Describe how star parallax is used to measure astronomical distances in light years. II

Explain and draw the Hertzsprung–Russell diagram, and use it to describe the possible stages in the evolution of a star. III

Explain how astronomical distances can be measured by knowing the apparent brightness and pulsation period of a Cepheid variable star. II

Describe the following components of the universe: stars, star clusters, nebulae, galaxies. II

Describe the dimensions of the Milky Way galaxy in light years, and locate our solar system within the Milky Way galaxy.   II

Describe the different types of galaxies in the universe, and explain their possible evolution.   II

04-010-030   Determine the mode of origin of specific rock types.   IV

Determine the relationships of temperature, pressure, and/or amount of water or ions free to move in the rock to the formation of metamorphic rock from described parent-rock environments. Include contact and regional metamorphism.   IV

Given samples, descriptions, rock identification charts, or sources, classify igneous, sedimentary, and metamorphic rocks.   II

Given information derived from igneous rocks (texture, grain size, color, or mineral content), draw conclusions about relative depth under the surface where the rock was formed, whether the rock was originally molten rock, and conditions under which the rock was formed.   IV

Given a description of the manner in which a certain rock was formed, determine whether the rock is metamorphic, sedimentary, or igneous.   III

Describe the history of the formation of an igneous rock in terms of its temperature and rate of cooling.   II

Describe the change in metamorphic rocks as a result of exposure to heat and pressure.   II

Classify metamorphic rocks as high-grade or low-grade metamorphism, according to Bowen's reaction series.   II

04-010-035   **Discuss the rock cycle in terms of the processes that act on the earth materials and the products that result.   III**

Show how the physical and chemical environments influence mineral formation by explaining the following phenomena.   II
1. The chemical composition of a diamond is the same as the chemical composition of graphite.
2. Alteration in the internal atomic arrangement of carbon, under specific conditions of heat and pressure, may result in formation of a diamond.
3. Pressure and temperature are two environmental factors that may cause one mineral to change to another.

Define *fracture, cleavage, streak, hardness, texture,* and *luster,* and explain the laboratory or field procedures that are used to determine these properties.   II

04-010-040   **Relate a mineral's properties to its atomic structure.   IV**

Define the terms *atoms, isotopes, ions, molecules, elements,* and *compounds,* and describe how they are related to minerals and rocks.   II

Discuss in what ways the following features are related: crystal, mineral, rock.   III

Explain elements and compounds in terms of atoms.   II

Describe how crystals of NaCl grow from a solution and the effect that rapid evaporation may have on the size of the crystals.   II

From a mineral tray, select distinctive minerals that can be identified by color and/or specific gravity.   I

04-010-045   **Discuss the composition of Earth, conditions under which various materials were formed, and the mechanisms for tectonic change.   III**

Given several conditions necessary for the formation of certain minerals and a list of minerals found in a particular area, recognize the environmental conditions that probably existed in that particular area.   II

Describe the chemical composition of Earth's three spheres: lithosphere, hydrosphere, and atmosphere.   II

Discuss the relative importance of elements, particularly oxygen, in each of the three Earth spheres.   III

Diagram and label a cross-sectional view of Earth (crust, mantle, outer core, and inner core).   II

Explain and diagram how depths to different rock layers can be determined by using seismic waves.   II

Describe one line of evidence that uplift of Earth's crust has taken place to form mountains.   II

Compare the permanent and the elastic deformation of a steel bar and a layer of rock.   III

Explain the mechanism of an earthquake in terms of permanent deformation of Earth's crust.   II

Explain a mechanism within Earth's mantle that accounts for mountains, earthquakes, and volcanoes.   II

Explain the theory of continental drift.   II

04-010-050   Identify changes that occur in the features of Earth, and relate the causes of these changes to the results.   IV

Given a description or illustration of a change in a feature of Earth, predict the agent that most likely produced the alteration. Agents of change include wind, water, volcanoes, meteorites, glaciers, landslides, and waves.   III

Given an experiment showing changes occurring across the interfaces of common objects, predict the following conditions.   III
1. What the changes are and where they occur
2. Which variables affect the rate (speed) at which these changes occur
3. How the experiment could be similar to natural changes on Earth's surfaces

Given examples of various agents of change, classify the agent as natural or man-made.   II

Given a description of weathered materials (natural or man-made) and a description of the original material, select the appropriate causes of such weathering.   II

Relate the development of mature soils from unweathered rock to the passing of time, movement of minerals and organic colloids, and depth of transformation.   IV

Given an erosional agent (water, wind, ice), relate the effects of gravity and kinetic energy to the erosion of different types of material.   II

Given the rate of current flow and the size of various particles being transported, predict the settling rates and graded bedding.   III

Differentiate between relevant and irrelevant facts associated with a hypothesis explaining geosyncline formation.   III

Given a diagram or description of a geosyncline, identify the locations of sedimentary rocks, name the types of deformation present, and interpret possible means of the geosyncline deformation.   II

Interpret continental profile maps, graphs, or illustrations that show depth and/or region relationships of volcanic chains, deep-sea trenches, mountains, and earthquake activity.   III

Describe relationships between areas of earthquake activity, mountain regions, ocean trenches, island arcs, and volcanoes.   II

04-010-055   Perceive relationships of the various factors that create weather conditions.   IV

Relate Earth's distance from the sun to the simultaneous existence of water in the gaseous, liquid, and solid states.   II

Identify how water-cycle processes of condensation, sublimation, precipitation, and melting are dependent upon energy transfer.   I

Identify appropriate cloud formations necessary to produce the following forms of precipitation: rain, hail, sleet, snow. I

Tell how air masses are created and how they supply the energy needed for development of cyclones along a polar front. I

On an outline map of the world, identify the following major climatic regions: polar ice cap, tundra (polar wet), taiga (subpolar wet), humid continental, humid subtropical, Marine West Coast, Mediterranean, steppe and desert (continental dry), savanna, tropical (rain forest). I

On an outline map of Africa, identify the following climatic regions: Mediterranean, semiarid (steppe), arid (desert), tropical wet and dry (savanna), tropical wet (rain forest), humid subtropical. I

Predict weather conditions from data relating to air temperature, pressure, and wind. III

On an outline map of Africa that identifies circulation patterns, predict the climatic characteristics of the following patterns: January winds, July winds, ocean currents III

04-010-060 **Show your understanding of the observational data used by meteorologists in predicting weather. II**

Explain the difference between weather and climate, and describe the atmospheric conditions characteristic of each. II

Given drawings or descriptions of these cloud formations, identify basic cloud types: cumulus, cirrus, stratus. I

Identify appropriate cloud formations necessary to produce the following forms of precipitation: rain, hail, sleet, snow. II

Match the different forms of precipitation with a description of how each is formed: rain, sleet, hail, snow. I

Recognize the four kinds of weather fronts, given a description or an example of each: warm, cold, stationary, occluded. II

Recognize the definitions of destructive forces of weather, given a description or diagram of each storm: thunderstorm, cyclone, typhoon, hurricane, tornado. II

Record your observations of elements of weather for a period of two weeks; record reports from the weather bureau for any information you cannot observe yourself. II

04-010-065 **Apply a knowledge of the characteristics of fronts to make weather predictions, including these weather elements: temperature, barometric pressure, cloud cover, precipitation, wind velocity. III**

Define an air mass, name the six most common types, and identify weather elements characteristic of each. I

Describe how the prevailing wind systems affect the movement of air masses and influence weather conditions. II

Identify four kinds of weather fronts on the basis of these characteristics: slope of front, wind direction, average velocity of the front, precipitation and associated clouds, relative barometric pressure, and temperatures of air masses. I

Explain what temperature is, show how it is measured by a thermometer and a thermograph, and record temperature on a weather-station model. II

Explain what barometric pressure is, measure it by using a mercury barometer, an aneroid barometer and a barograph, and record it on a weather-station model, converting inches of mercury to millibars as necessary. II

Explain what humidity is, and demonstrate the relationship between temperature and moisture capacity. III

Calculate, using a sling psychrometer and appropriate charts, the moisture content of air, relative humidity, and absolute humidity, and find the dew point and record it on a weather-station model. II

List the products of condensation and precipitation, and describe the effect of temperature on their formation. II

Diagram and use the cloud classification system to describe cloud types, and record the percentage of cloud cover on a weather-station model. III

Explain the origin of local high- and low-pressure systems and local winds. II

Draw the appropriate isobars between stations, given the barometric pressure at different weather stations. III

Diagram and explain the flow of air around high- and low-pressure systems. III

Read wind velocity, using an anemometer, and record wind velocity on a weather-station model. I

04-010-070 **Discuss the relationships between changes in temperature and pressure, and changes in solar heating with respect to their effect on weather conditions. III**

Describe the nature of Earth's atmosphere and the layer closest to Earth, the troposphere. I

List, with percentages, the two most abundant gases in the troposphere, and explain the importance of the minor gases in the study of meteorology. II

Explain the effect of heat energy on molecular motion and the way that changes in molecular motion result in changes in the state of a substance. II

Explain how solar energy heats the air in the troposphere through conduction, convection, and radiation, and explain the nature of the greenhouse effect. II

Recognize and use the formula $\frac{PV}{T} = K$ to predict changes in gases, particularly in air, when any of the three factors—temperature, pressure, and volume—are varied. II

Describe the change in the molecular concentration of air caused by an external change in temperature as well as the changes caused by an internal or adiabatic change. II

Explain how water-cycle processes of condensation, sublimation, precipitation, and melting are dependent upon energy transfer. II

Explain the distribution of solar energy according to latitude. II

Explain the origin of the equatorial low-pressure and the polar high-pressure areas that result from unequal heating. II

Diagram and explain the formation of three cells of atmospheric circulation over each hemisphere. II

Diagram and explain the flow of the prevailing winds on the surface of a nonrotating Earth, and describe the Coriolis effect on the flow of air on the surface as Earth rotates. II

Name, diagram, and explain the flow of the prevailing winds on the surface of a rotating Earth.   II

04-010-075 **Show your understanding of hydrology by predicting the availability of water in particular areas.   III**

Identify the various forms in which moisture reaches Earth's surface and the ways in which this moisture is stored. I

Define *percolation, porosity,* and *permeability,* and show how porosity and permeability may be calculated. II

Considering porosity, water retention, and permeability, explain the relationship of soil-particle size to the formation of capillary and gravity water. III

Define *evapotranspiration rate,* and identify three methods that can be used to measure it.   I

Given the potential evapotranspiration rate (PE) and the amount of moisture supplied to a geographic region by precipitation, suggest the water deficiency or surplus and the amount of vegetation in that area.   II

Given the necessary data and a graph that shows the water budget for a geographic region, describe three factors that affect the water budget in that area.   III

Diagram and label the free and artesian groundwater systems.   III

Explain the process by which calcite is chemically decomposed by groundwater, and show how this process relates to the formation of caves and sinkholes.   II

Identify sinkholes, groundwater lakes, and swamps on a topographic map.   I

04-010-080   Show your understanding of the nature of the sea–air interface.   II

Given discrepancies in salinity content within the hydrologic cycle, identify the possible sources (causes) of such changes.   I

Identify the physical and chemical properties of the sea or atmosphere that affect matter and energy transfer across the sea–air interface.   II

Explain the importance of solar energy to the formation of ocean waves and currents.   II

Label the parts of a wave, and compare the movement of wave energy and the movement of water molecules in the wave.   I

List five agents responsible for wave formation.   I

Describe the changes that take place in a wave as cresting occurs and the relationship of undertow to cresting.   II

Describe the process of wave refraction and the formation of longshore current. II

Recognize the following erosional and depositional forms shown on topographic maps: sea stack, sea cliff, spit, beach. II

04-010-085 **Given an erosional agent (water, wind, ice), relate the effects of gravity and kinetic energy to the erosion of different types of material. IV**

Given a description of weathered materials (natural or man-made) and a description of the original material, predict the probable causes of weathering. III

Relate the development of mature soils from unweathered rock to the passing of time, movement of minerals and organic colloids, and depth of transformation. IV

Recognize the processes and products of the hydrologic cycle and explain their relationship to solar energy and gravity. II

Derive the relationship between the energy of a stream and its mass and velocity, using the energy equation. IV

Explain vertical and lateral erosion of streambeds, and show how each energy system is related to the formation of steep or shallow valleys. II

Describe stream equilibrium, using the scale balance model, and explain how changes in slope, discharge, sediment load, and sediment size can cause a stream to erode or deposit. II

Given the rate of current flow and the size of various particles transported, make inferences about settling rates and graded bedding. IV

04-010-090 **Using descriptions of environments, biome maps, and climatogram information, determine the probable distribution of living things in a given environment. IV**

Given a description of an environment, recognize which conditions are the major determiners of the types of organisms that can survive in that environment. II

From biome maps and climatogram information, recognize the major abiotic environmental factors that determine a specific biome type.   II

Identify the general biotic conditions that are common to most biomes.   I

Determine the methods that humans have used or could use to transform a specific biome, making the biome more adaptable to their way of life.   IV

Conduct an experiment to test variables you have selected that affect the rate of decomposition of organic materials.   III

04-010-095   Predict the success of various methods of preventing and controlling pollution.   III

Identify the major sources of environmental pollution.   I

Describe the effect of specific chemical pollutants on living and nonliving matter in the environment.   II

Explain how pollution can change an environment.   II

Explain how a particular source of pollution may have primary and secondary effects.   II

04-010-100   Discuss the work done by a group of scientists on sediment dating and radioactive-clock methods of dating. Analyze how their results clarify the mechanisms involved in the decline of one group of animals and the increase in another group of animals.   IV

Given the general results of work by scientists, infer whether the work contributes to the geologic record of life in the past or to a theory explaining the origin of life.   IV

Describe sediment dating and radioactive-clock methods of dating fossils.   II

Given a chart that illustrates evolutionary relationships of organisms, recognize the common ancestors of different organisms.   II

Identify the factors that eventually led to a decline in the dominance of amphibians and reptiles and to an increase in the dominance of mammals. I

04-010-105 **Demonstrate your ability to perceive relationships in a laboratory experiment by making inferences and predictions based upon quantitative results that you have tabulated and graphed. IV**

Given a statement of the observations from an experiment, classify each observation as qualitative or quantitative. II

Given the results of a laboratory procedure (experiment), record the results and display them in tabular and graphic form. II

Interpret the factual information displayed in a graph. II

Explain the way two variables on a graph of biological data are related. II

Analyze and discuss results of an experiment that have been expressed graphically. IV

Record observations of an experiment, and draw inferences that are supported by the data. IV

Given a description of a scientific experiment, summarize the information into a complete laboratory report that includes title, problem, hypothesis, procedure, data, and conclusion. II

04-010-110 **Make predictions based on your analysis of laboratory observations and measurements stated in a table or in graph form, using either interpolation or extrapolation. (Interpolation: predicting between two points; extrapolation: predicting beyond the last known point.) IV**

Given descriptions of particular attitudes or beliefs, differentiate between attitudes or beliefs formed after scientific observation and those based upon previously formed or untested beliefs. III

Given a table or graph of the results of an experiment, (1) interpret the results, (2) make predictions based upon the results, and (3) determine whether the results support, refute, or have no bearing upon the hypothesis tested.   IV

Given an example of a graph, make inferences and predictions based upon information presented in graphical form.   IV

Explain how a geologist can predict past environmental conditions on the basis of the type of minerals present in any particular area.   II

04-010-115   Combine concepts, principles, and generalizations by designing and conducting an experiment to test the validity of a given hypothesis and by analyzing and reporting the results.   V

Given a scientific event or situation, suggest questions that help explain the event or situation.   II

Given a question, the answer to which would help explain a scientific event or situation, suggest sources of information or activities that may lead to an answer to the question.   II

Make an inference from a set of observations.   IV

Develop a hypothesis based on observations and inferences. (A hypothesis is an idea stated in such a way that it can be tested.)   V

Given a hypothesis that can be tested, design a laboratory procedure (experiment) that will test the hypothesis.   V

Identify variables that affect an experiment in earth science. (Variables are the parts of an experiment that are deliberately changed or kept from changing to see what effect they have in the experiment.)   I

Determine how a variable may affect an experiment in earth science.   IV

Physics

04-015-005 **Given a brief history of the development of a physical law, discuss the law's history by indicating the period of time that the law was first a hypothesis, the period that the hypothesis became a theory, and the period that the theory was recognized as a law. III**

Differentiate between fact and theory. III

Define *hypothesis, theory,* and *law.* I

04-015-010 **Explain physical and chemical properties and changes. II**

Given a description of a physical or chemical change, conclude the effect of a specific manipulated variable on that change. II

Given a series of situations in which change has taken place, describe the physical changes and the chemical changes. II

Given a chemical change, suggest variables that could affect the change. II

Given a list of specific properties of a substance, classify each property as physical or chemical. II

Given the name of a metal and/or a description of its properties, explain why it could or could not be used for a given purpose. II

Given the name of a gas and/or a description of its properties, explain why it could or could not be used for a given purpose. II

04-015-015 **Make measurements and calculations with respect to time, distance, area, and volume as required in word problems and express results in scientific notation. III**

Using scientific (exponential) notation, solve given word problems that involve measurements of time and require calculations and/or experiments. III

Solve given word problems that involve measurements of distance, area, and volume and that require calculations and/or experiments. Express results in significant figures. III

04-015-020 Use the metric system of measurement by applying the system in all scientific experiments performed during the year. IV

Identify the basic metric unit that is used for measuring each of the following: length, weight, volume, temperature. I

Define each of the prefixes used to indicate different units of measure in the metric system (*milli-, centi-, deci-, kilo-*). Given a measure of length, volume, or weight in any metric unit, convert the measure to any other metric unit of length, volume, or weight. III

Measure the length of objects in metric units to within 0.1 centimeter (cm). III

Measure the volume of solids and liquids in metric units to within 1 milliliter (ml). III

Calculate the volume of rectangular solids to within 0.1 cubic centimeter (cc). III

Measure the weight of objects in metric units to within 0.1 gram (gm). III

Measure temperatures to within 1°C or 1°F. III

Record as many observations as possible. Record all measurements in metric-system terms. III

Given a number less than 100,000, express the number to three significant figures. Given an extremely large or small number, express it in scientific notation (exponential notation). Given the range of uncertainty (± principle) of an instrument and a reading from that instrument, write a corrected expression for that reading. II

04-015-025   **Discuss the relative positions of stationary and moving objects. III**

Describe the direction of movement that an object has as seen by another observer relative to the position of that observer. The description could include reference to another object or system. II

Recognize evidence of motion in photographs, motion pictures, or flip-book pictures by reporting differential speeds of pictured objects that have apparent motion. Identify changes in the position of pictured objects relative to specified reference objects. II

Given illustrations of two objects or systems that have different rates of motion, recognize which object or system is moving faster and which is moving slower. II

04-015-030   **Identify the phases of matter, discuss the changes at the molecular level, and describe the properties at each phase. III**

Given a property of matter, define the property and classify it into one of the following groups: general properties, specific properties, physical properties, chemical properties. II

Demonstrate one way to show that matter takes up space. III

Demonstrate one way to show that matter has weight. III

Differentiate between weight and mass. III

Recognize several properties of an object or a substance, including color, shape, size, texture, taste, odor, and state of matter. Recognize the sense used to determine each of these properties. II

Explain how plasma differs from solids, liquids, and gases. Given a list of substances, recognize those that are plasma. II

Given a situation in which an object or substance must fit into a prescribed space or conform to a stated weight capacity, explain whether it is more important to know about the material's weight or its volume.   II

Given a list of substances, identify each substance as a gas, a liquid, or a solid.   I

Describe a solid, a liquid, and a gas in terms of definite or indefinite volume and shape.   II

Explain the relative motion of the molecules and the relative distances between the molecules in the solid, liquid, and gaseous phases of matter.   II

Identify the points of phase change and describe the processes involved: boiling, boiling point, freezing, freezing point, melting, melting point, sublimation, condensation, vaporization.   II

04-015-035   Discuss the relationships between mass, volume, and density.   III

Explain the difference between the operational definitions of *weight* and *mass.*   II

Given the formula $V = l \times w \times h$, find the volume of a regular solid such as a rectangular prism, using the basic metric unit of volume, the cubic centimeter.   II

Given information on the mass and volume of various objects, describe how mass, volume, and density are related.   II

04-015-040   Given a description or a diagram, discuss atoms, elements, molecules, compounds, and mixtures.   III

Given illustrations or models of different substances, identify the substance illustrated as an element, an atom, a compound, or a mixture.   I

From a given definition or description of a substance, recognize the substance as a compound or a mixture.   II

Given a model that represents a molecule of a compound, select the formula that matches the model.   I

Define the terms *matter, molecule, atom, electron,* and *neutron.*   I

Given a list of early theories on matter, match each theory with the scientist who furthered it: Dalton, Boyle, Democritus, Empedocles.   I

Interpret information obtained from simple experimental tests to identify elements.   II

Explain the difference between an atom and a molecule, given a diagram, drawing, or description of each.   II

Given a model or formula for a molecule, determine the number of atoms and elements in the molecule represented.   III

Classify common substances as elements or compounds, given symbols, formulas, or models.   II

Classify substances (e.g., sugar, salt, glass) as crystalline or noncrystalline, given a description or drawing of the molecular arrangements.   II

04-015-045   Construct a model of an element to show the relationship between the atomic number of the element and the number of electrons in an atom of the element.   III

Recognize the relationship between the atomic number of an element and the number of electrons in the atom of the element.   II

Given atomic models of isotopes of the same element, identify the parts and tell how the models differ.   I

04-015-050   Given a demonstration of a moving object, use these terms to explain the phenomena: force, inertia, energy, work, friction.   III

Identify acceptable definitions for the terms *force, inertia,* and *weight.*   I

Demonstrate your understanding of the term *force* and apply the term in describing situations where push or pull is exerted on an object.   III

From observation of an experiment, recognize proof that to act against a certain gravitational force (weight) requires an equal amount of force.   II

Recognize examples of inertia shown in experiments.   II

Identify the variables that affect the swing of a pendulum, and tell how the swing is affected by those variables.   I

From a list of common objects, recognize those that are in a state of potential energy (stored energy) and those that are in a state of kinetic energy (energy of motion).   II

Explain what form of energy (mechanical, chemical, heat, light, sound, electrical) and/or what state of energy (kinetic or potential) different objects have, use, or produce that make it possible for them to do work.   II

Given a description of an energy change, explain whether it has been a transformation in the form or the state of the energy and/or name the form or state to which it has been changed.   II

Given a situation showing inertia of different objects, describe factors (size, shape, mass) that affect the inertia of an object.   II

04-015-055   Combine concepts, principles, and generalizations by developing relationships among the various properties of objects moving in space.   V

Given a table of the positions of an object at various times, represent the following on graphs: position versus time, average velocity versus time, average acceleration versus time.   III

Given a graph of the position of an object moving in a line versus time, represent the following on a table: position versus time, velocity versus time, acceleration versus time.   III

Given a table of the positions of an object at various times, find the x, y, and z components of the average velocity between those points.   III

From a set of component velocities or accelerations, find the resultant velocity or acceleration.   III

04-015-060   **Combine concepts, principles, and generalizations by designing three experiments that show the increase or decrease of the speed of an object and velocity as a function of time.   V**

Given a description or an illustration of a situation that involves an object rolling or sliding from one surface to another, predict whether the speed of the object will increase or decrease and whether a change in direction is likely to occur.   III

Given a description of an object changing velocity, construct a graph that shows velocity as a function of time, and predict changes in velocity with respect to time. Explain positive acceleration and negative acceleration or deceleration.   III

04-015-065   **Demonstrate the properties of force and the ways in which properties interact.   III**

Given a description of a force, classify the force as a vector or a scalar quantity.   II

Identify three pre-Galilean concepts of force, and list the empirical support for each concept.   I

Given a description of three simultaneous forces acting in a plane on an object, find the x and y components of the resultant force on the object.   III

Given a written description of a series of forces applied to an object of mass M, find its velocity in three dimensions after each force is applied.   III

Explain the difference between inertial mass and active and passive gravitational mass, and the difference between mass and weight.   II

Describe the various forces found in nature, explaining the distances over which the forces act, their strength, and the quantities (such as mass) on which they depend. Include frictional, gravitational, electrical, magnetic, and nuclear forces.   III

Calculate the gravitational forces acting between two massive bodies.   III

04-015-070   Given a simple machine, demonstrate its mechanical advantages and devise a simple tool of your own.   V

Describe ways that the following simple machines make work easier: inclined plane, fixed pulley, wheel and axle, level, wedge, screw.   II

Given drawings of levers, recognize the fulcrum, the load, and the best point to apply effort.   II

Demonstrate the difference between the values of a fixed pulley and of a block and tackle as simple machines.   III

Demonstrate relationships between effort applied and amount of work done in experimental situations by using simple machines.   III

Design a simple tool to perform a task related to work or study.   V

Given descriptions or illustrations of examples of levers, classify each as an example of a first-, second-, or third-class lever.   II

Given any two of the following three variables, solve for the unknown: resistance, force, actual mechanical advantage.   II

Given the clockwise and counterclockwise moments or the forces and distances needed to calculate the moments of a lever (first-, second-, or third-class), apply the Law of Moments to state the rotational direction of the lever.   III

Given seesaw word problems that include any three of the following, apply the appropriate principle and solve the problem: distance to the load, distance to the effort, amount of load, amount of effort. III

Given the amounts of force required to move a load and the distance of the load from the fulcrum for a first- and a second-class lever, construct a graph for each. Given the amount of force required to move a load and the distance of the force from the fulcrum for a third-class lever, construct a graph. III

Given a word problem containing a description of a task to be accomplished by using a lever, predict whether the task can be done. III

04-015-075 **Combine concepts, principles, and generalizations about Newton's basic laws by designing a simple experiment that illustrates their application. Develop a hypothesis, test it with variables, draw conclusions, and make generalizations. V**

Given a series of everyday activities, recognize those that are dependent upon gravitational force. II

Predict how the following factors affect the movement of objects: forces, friction, unbalanced forces. V

Design a simple experiment that demonstrates the application of Newton's First Law of Motion (Law of Inertia). V

Predict what will happen to objects in motion or at rest when some force is applied to the objects. III

Predict which of several objects will accelerate most, given the mass of the objects and the size and direction of the force applied. III

Match each of the following terms with its definition: *motion, friction, mass.* I

Given a definition or example of *speed, acceleration, velocity, inertia,* or *momentum,* match each term to its definition or example. I

Given a description of a commonplace situation, such as the sudden braking of a car, explain how Newton's laws of motion are illustrated.   II

Explain how the gravitational force between two masses is affected by changes in the masses or by changes in the distance between the masses, and solve related problems.   III

04-015-080   Analyze the relationships expressed in the conservation laws, and solve problems utilizing these laws.   IV

Given an impulse applied to a stationary mass, calculate its subsequent velocity and momentum.   II

Using the law of the conservation of momentum, solve word problems concerning head-on collisions between two masses.   III

Find the quantity of kinetic energy given to an object from the amount of work performed on the object. Explain the difference between work and force.   III

Find the amount of potential energy stored in compressed springs and in elevated objects.   III

Solve word problems involving colliding or falling bodies, using the law of conservation of energy.   III

Given a description of a mechanical event, such as the launching of a satellite, support an explanation of the event in terms of the laws of conservation of energy and momentum.   III

04-015-085   Explain the processes by which nuclear energy is produced, and evaluate the benefits in relation to the possible negative effects.   VI

Given a description of an atom before and after a nuclear process has occurred, explain whether the atom went through natural radioactive decay, artificial radioactive decay (fission), or fusion.   II

Describe the beneficial aspects of nuclear energy (e.g., treatment of cancer) and the detrimental aspects (e.g., radioactive fallout). II

Describe three uses of nuclear materials in medicine. II

04-015-090 Demonstrate the effects of heat on matter. Describe the effects in terms of molecular change. III

Read a thermometer to the nearest degree in either °F or °C. II

Identify the boiling and freezing points of water on both the Fahrenheit scale and the centigrade scale. I

Demonstrate the boiling points of various water solutions. III

Using the terms *expand* or *contract,* describe the state to which matter changes when heat energy is added or taken away. II

Given two states of matter, tell whether heat must be added or taken away to go from the first to the second state, and name the process involved. I

Given a description or illustration of a change of state of a liquid, explain whether the temperature of the substance was at the freezing point or the boiling point. II

Conduct an experiment to demonstrate the cause-and-effect relationship between temperature and the time it takes for a substance to dissolve in water. Use the following steps. III
1. Hypothesis (guess of results based on previous observation and knowledge)
2. Design (steps you will take, material you will use)
3. Record of observations
4. Conclusions

Describe how heat affects the amount of solid substance that will dissolve in water. II

Given two states of matter, explain what occurs when heat is added or taken away. Explain what has happened to the molecules between the first and second state, and give the name of the process. II

Given a substance, explain the effect of heat on the volume of the substance and on the speed of the molecular action or motion.   II

Explain the difference between the scientific definitions of *heat* and of *temperature,* and use these terms in a sentence. II

Define *conduction, convection,* and *radiation.*   I

Explain the operation of the following devices in response to temperature changes: *thermostat, thermometer, thermocouple.* II

04-015-095 Interpret diagrams that illustrate the principles of sound. III

Use the molecular theory and wave theory to explain how sound travels from its source (or beginning) to the person who hears it.   III

Given an experiment in which different numbers of waves are produced, draw a diagram to demonstrate how the number of waves made per second (frequency) is related to the amount of force that is required to make them. III

Given an experiment and a diagram showing the results of the experiment, recognize the relationship between the amplitude (height and depth) of the waves and the force it took to make those waves. II

Tell what conditions are needed for making and hearing sounds. I

Given the number of seconds a sound takes to travel from its source to the hearer, determine the distance traveled through the air by the sound. III

Given a list of materials or substances that transmit sound, identify those that carry sound waves well and those that are poor conductors. I

Given a description of the surface of a material, tell whether the surface will take in sound (absorb it) or echo (reflect) it. I

Conduct an experiment that demonstrates the relationship between expended energy and volume of sound. Change the amount of energy to vary the volume of sound produced. III

Recognize the relative volume of a series of sound (loudest or softest) when shown graphs picturing their amplitude or given data about the amplitude of volume. II

Tell how the pitch (frequency) of a sound can be raised or lowered when the length, thickness, or tension of the vibrating object is changed. I

04-015-100 Demonstrate the characteristics of wave motion. III

Describe transverse and longitudinal mechanical waves in a string or spring, and calculate the wavelength as a function of wave velocity and frequency. III

Discuss the principles of reinforcement as applied to waves that are reflected and to waves that are refracted around objects. III

Draw and discuss diagrams illustrating the superposition principle and the interference of waves. III

04-015-105 Combine concepts, principles, and generalizations by designing and presenting a demonstration of the nature and behavior of light. V

Define the terms *transparent, translucent,* and *opaque,* and give examples of objects with these characteristics. I

Explain how light and the parts of the eye interact to produce an image. II

Recognize which of the three most common theories about the nature of light is demonstrated in examples of the way light travels. II

Given information about the roughness or smoothness of some objects, recognize which objects will reflect light in a scattered way and which will reflect it in a regular way. II

Recognize whether substances or objects with different surface textures and colors will reflect or absorb most of the light that falls on them. II

Design an experiment to show whether substances or objects with different surface textures and colors reflect or absorb most of the light that falls on them. V

Predict the angle at which light will be reflected from a surface, given the angle at which that light strikes that surface. III

Recognize diagrams that illustrate how white light is bent (refracted) as it passes through concave and convex lenses, prisms, and water. II

Predict the kinds of images that will be made by convex lenses and the kinds made by concave lenses. III

04-015-110 **Make judgments that involve the characteristics of light waves. VI**

Compare the wave theory and particle theory of light. Include in your comparison an application of Snell's law, a discussion of the independent measurements of Foucault and Michelson to verify the wave theory, and a discussion of the role of the principle of refraction in both theories. VI

Present a theory about why interference effects are not normally seen in light. Using this theory and Thomas Young's experiment, determine wavelength from observed interference effects. Explain how your conclusions support the wave theory of light. IV

Given the interference pattern of a monochromatic light source, solve word problems related to the wavelength of that light. III

Write a paper in which you compare Huygens' wave model of light with diffraction phenomena, particularly as applied to diffraction gratings. Determine the wavelength of incident light from the optical geometry of a transmission grating. VI

04-015-115 Analyze the relationships expressed in the quantum theory of light by solving problems utilizing this theory. IV

Explain the development of the electromagnetic theory of light from Faraday to Hertz. Given the general character of electromagnetic radiations, classify the radiations in the eight major regions of the electromagnetic spectrum. II

Explain the three laws of photoelectric emission. Describe to what extent a wave model of light is successful in explaining these laws. II

Recognize the definition of the quantities in Einstein's photoelectric equation. Describe the significance of the photoelectric effect and the assumptions of Planck. II

Given Planck's relationship describing the energy of a photon radiated at frequency f from some source and Einstein's equation for mass-energy equivalency, derive an equation for the momentum associated with that photon in terms of its wavelength. IV

04-015-120 Present the evidence for modern theories concerning wavelike properties of particles of matter. III

Present in an outline the experimental support for de Broglie's proposal that particles of matter have wavelike properties associated with them. III

Describe the significance of the de Broglie relation by explaining the behavior of a particle of small kinetic energy moving in or near an atom. II

Recognize three major characteristics of subatomic particles that enable man to detect the presence of these particles. Describe the operation of instruments or devices that can be used to detect these particles.   II

Identify the differences between Van de Graaff generators, circular accelerators, and linear accelerators in relation to types of particles accelerated, particle energies attainable, operation, and current use.   I

Identify fundamental subatomic particles as baryons, mesons, or leptons. List three conservation laws that apply to the nuclear interactions of these particles.   I

Express the principle of symmetry and the law of parity. Describe the connection between the two concepts. Describe the experimental failure of the theory of conservation of parity.   II

04-015-125   Analyze the relationships expressed in the kinetic theory of gases and solve problems utilizing this theory.   IV

Solve word problems concerning the amount of heat energy in given bodies at various temperatures and problems concerning the exchange of heat between various bodies.   III

Use the kinetic theory of matter to describe molecular motion of the different phases of matter.   III

Describe the relationship between the molecular theory of gases and Boyle's law. Solve word problems, using Boyle's law.   III

Describe the relationship between the ideal gas law and the kinetic theory of gases. Solve word problems, using the ideal gas law.   III

Find the amount of positive or negative work done by a gas that expands or contracts relative to its surroundings during adiabatic and isothermal processes.   III

Using Bernoulli's law, solve word problems and answer questions concerning moving fluids.   III

04-015-130 **Describe the internal-combustion engine in terms of potential, kinetic, electrical, chemical, and mechanical energy. II**

Given drawings that show movement of air or water molecules, recognize which illustrates the greater production of kinetic energy. II

Given a description of machine activities that show different forms of energy (mechanical, chemical, or electrical), match each machine activity with the form of energy that it uses or produces. I

Given a description of an internal-combustion engine, recognize where potential, kinetic, chemical, or mechanical energy is being used or produced. II

04-015-135 **Analyze the relationships between electric charges and electric current under various conditions. IV**

Given a description of two kinds of electric charges and the forces between them, explain how these forces can be understood in terms of charged particles in atoms. II

Given a description of the behavior of an electroscope, explain the electrostatic-induction phenomenon in terms of charged particles in atoms. II

Explain how the electroscope can be refined and used for accurate quantitative measurements. II

Using a battery as an example of a device for separating electrical charges, draw a diagram and describe how this charge separation can result in an electric current. III

Define *electric current.* I

Prepare a table of electrical conductivity according to state, temperature, and material. III

Define and explain the behavior of charged bodies in terms of Coulomb's law. II

Using Coulomb's law, solve problems that involve electrical forces between two charges. III

Use Millikan's oil-drop experiment as a basis for measuring the constant of proportionality in Coulomb's law.   III

Calculate the mass of an electron or a proton, given the speed attained by either particle in traversing a known distance.   III

Using a qualitative definition of electric current in terms of moving elementary charges, describe how currents can be measured by electrolysis.   II

Perform an experiment to verify the following assumptions by measuring the kinetic energy of a beam of moving charges.   III
1. All elementary charges are the same.
2. The force on a moving charge is independent of its speed.

Describe electric field and potential difference in terms of interactions between elementary charged particles.   II

Using the concepts of electric field and potential difference, define open and closed circuits and describe methods of measuring potential differences.   II

Describe electric circuits from the viewpoint of kinetic energy and charged particles. Solve problems, using Ohm's law.   III

04-015-140 List the components of an electric circuit, and compare them with those of a simple hydraulic system.   IV

List the fundamental atomic particles, and diagram the Bohr model of the atom.   III

Explain the role of the electron in carrying electricity.   II

Define an ion and describe the process of ionization.   II

Differentiate between random drift of free electrons and the directed drift that constitutes current flow.   III

Diagram a complete (closed) circuit, and draw a schematic diagram of a simple circuit containing a power source, a load, a switch, and conductor wires.   III

Diagram the direction of current flow in a circuit in terms of both conventional notation and modern electron theory. III

Define a coulomb as the basic unit of electron charge. I

Define an ampere as a rate—coulombs of charge per second—and calculate current from this basic relationship. III

Write the common symbols for current, charge, and time, as distinguished from the standard (SI) abbreviations for their units of measure. III

List the steps for placing a simple ammeter, and connect an ammeter into a circuit to measure current. II

04-015-145 **Discuss two kinds of potential difference, voltage rise and voltage drop, and describe the symbols used to differentiate them. III**

Define electromotive force (emf) in terms of Coulomb's law of charged bodies. I

Explain potential difference in terms of electrical pressure. II

Define emf and potential difference as separate forms of the same force, and define voltage as the measure of potential difference. I

Explain how voltage represents work done in an electric circuit. II

Calculate voltage from the basic definition of the volt as joules per coulomb of charge moved through the circuit. II

Describe how the dry cell produces emf by converting chemical energy to electrical energy. II

Explain the process of separating charges in a battery. II

Diagram a series connection and a parallel connection of cells in terms of the resulting total voltage. III

Explain how an opposing voltage affects total output voltage.   II

Explain where voltage can be measured in an electric circuit.   II

Connect a voltmeter in a circuit to make voltage measurements.   III

04-015-150   Connect an ohmmeter in a circuit to make resistance measurements.   III

Name the parameters that vary resistance values.   I

Calculate resistance of a wire, given its resistivity and dimensions.   II

Describe the effects of temperature on resistance.   II

List the uses of resistance, and describe the classes of resistors and the circuit symbols that represent them.   II

Identify resistor ratings and the codes by which they are designated.   I

04-015-155   Discuss the relation between voltage drop across a resistor and the ohmic value of its resistance.   III

Explain a series circuit.   II

Describe how a parallel circuit differs from a series circuit.   II

Use a multimeter to measure current in a series circuit.   III

State Kirchhoff's voltage law.   I

Use a multimeter to measure voltage in a direct-current (dc) circuit.   III

Make alternating-current (ac) voltage measurements.   III

04-015-160 **Demonstrate that varying the resistance affects current in a series circuit in which the voltage is held constant. III**

Explain how varying the voltage affects current in a series circuit in which the resistance is held constant. II

Present a verbal statement of Ohm's law. III

State the mathematical form of Ohm's law. I

Calculate values in a series circuit, using the Ohm's law formula. II

Derive several forms of the power equation from the basic power equation and Ohm's law. III

Calculate power expended in a series circuit. II

List the effects of source internal resistance. I

Describe how internal resistance can be determined. II

Define *short circuit* and *open circuit.* I

Explain how to locate a short circuit by using an ohmmeter or a voltmeter. II

Explain how to locate an open circuit by using an ohmmeter or a voltmeter. II

04-015-165 **Use variational analysis as a tool in understanding how circuit quantities interact. III**

Define *parallel circuit.* I

Describe the relation of source voltage to parallel branches. II

Explain the relation of source current and branch currents. II

State Kirchhoff's current law. I

Calculate source and branch currents, using Ohm's law. II

Calculate total circuit resistance.   II

Reduce complex circuit schematics to simple form by redrawing.   III

Use a multimeter to troubleshoot parallel circuits.   III

Explain how a parallel circuit is fused.   II

04-015-170   Determine quantities in a complex circuit by applying basic theories of electricity.   IV

Analyze a series-parallel circuit.   IV

Calculate total resistance in a complex circuit.   II

Practice complex circuit reduction by redrawing.   III

Solve for power in complex circuits.   III

Define *voltage reference*.   I

Define *ground* and *floating ground*.   I

Explain how a voltage divider works.   II

Construct a voltage divider.   III

04-015-175   Discuss the relationship between electricity and magnetism.   III

List the properties of a magnetic field, and state the laws governing magnetic fields.   I

Define the three types of magnetism, and identify the types of magnetic materials.   I

Explain how magnetic shielding works.   II

State the magnetic-domain theory.   I

Distinguish between the various types of magnets.   III

Define and illustrate the *left-hand rule for conductors.*
III

Diagram the magnetic-field around a current-carrying
loop. III

Diagram a magnetic field around a coil. III

Define and illustrate the *left-hand rule for coils.* III

Describe how a solenoid and a relay work. II

List the factors affecting flux density in an inductor. I

State and interpret Lenz's law. III

State the principles of electromagnetic induction. I

List the factors affecting generated emf. I

**04-015-180 Analyze the relationships between magnetic fields and
the currents producing them. IV**

Describe the sources and nature of magnetic fields and
the relationship of the magnetic field strength to the
current producing the field. II

For a current in a magnetic field, calculate the direction
of the force exerted on the current relative to the
direction of the current and of the magnetic field. Relate
the magnitude of the magnetic force to the magnitude,
force field, and force vector of the electric current. III

Assuming that the force on a current is the sum of the
forces on the elementary particles of which the current
is composed, apply the scientific principle involved to
development of an expression for the force exerted by
a magnetic field on a moving charged particle. III

Describe how masses of charged particles can be
measured by accelerating the masses to a known energy
with a magnetic field perpendicular to their velocity.
Describe how interacting magnetic and electric fields
can be used to identify fast-moving charged particles. II

Use the concept of circulation of the magnetic field around the current producing the field to describe the magnetic field at a distance r from a long straight wire. Explain how Ampere's circuital law applies to this situation.   II

By experimentation, find the constant in the circulation law and state complete equations for the magnetic field produced by various current configurations.   III

04-015-185   Demonstrate the principles of electromagnetic induction.   III

Define *mutual induction.*   I

Find the direction of the induced emf in a conductor.   III

Differentiate between induction and inductance.   III

Name the units of inductance.   I

State the rules for solving for total-inductance problems.   I

Tell how mutual induction takes place between two coils.   I

Graph the behavior of an idealized *RL* circuit.   III

Plot current rise, resistor voltage, and coil voltage in an *RL* circuit from opening of the switch (time $T = 0$) until steady state.   III

Plot decay of current, collapse of flux lines, and decay of voltage in an *RL* circuit from opening of the switch (time $T = 0$) until steady state.   III

Define the *RL* constant.   I

Make calculations, using the universal time-constant chart.   III

Recognize how Faraday's experiments dealing with a loop moving through a magnetic field contributed to the concept of magnetic flux.   II

Explain the relationship between the induced emf in a conductor and the rate of change of the magnetic flux. II

Describe how an electric field can be induced by a changing magnetic flux. Describe how the principles of electricity and magnetism make possible the prediction that electric and magnetic fields can propel themselves through space. II

04-015-190 **List the physical factors in a capacitor that affect its capacitance, and derive an equation for capacitance from these physical factors. III**

Explain what a capacitor does. II

Describe how a capacitor charges and discharges. II

List and describe the kinds of capacitors. II

Explain how a capacitor charges in an *RC* circuit. II

Explain how a capacitor discharges in an *RC* circuit. II

Define *capacitance;* then define *unit of capacitance* in terms of the basic quantities used to define capacitance, and calculate capacitance from this relationship. II

Calculate the value of total capacitance for capacitors in series. II

Calculate the value of total capacitance for capacitors in parallel. II

Calculate the value of total capacitance for capacitors in series-parallel. II

Define the *RC* time constant. I

Calculate the *RC* time constant from the basic formula. II

Solve *RC* time-constant problems, using the universal time-constant chart. III

04-015-195 Discuss the uses of ac and dc power. III

> Describe how ac voltage is generated. II

> Describe an ac wave, and demonstrate the graphing of an ac wave. III

> Name the parts of an ac generator. I

> Describe the functions of slip rings and a commutator. II

04-015-200 Demonstrate the phase relationship between current and voltage in an inductive ac circuit. III

> Describe how a coil reacts to ac. II

> Define *inductive reactance,* and explain the factors affecting it. II

> Calculate inductive reactance and the current in an inductive circuit. II

> Define *vector,* and find the sum of two vectors. III

> Graph a sine wave from a rotating vector. III

> Define *capacitive reactance,* and explain the factors affecting capacitive reactance. II

> Calculate capacitive reactance, and explain the phase relationships between current and voltage in a capacitive ac circuit. III

> Add ac voltages graphically; then add ac voltages vectorially. III

> Define *impedance* and calculate it. II

> Define *real power, apparent power, reactive power,* and *power factor.* I

> Compute the power factor. III

> Solve the power triangle. III

04-015-205 **Determine the direction of induced voltage in the secondary conditions. IV**

Explain the function of a transformer, and describe how a transformer is constructed and its uses. II

Draw the schematic of a transformer with more than one secondary winding. III

Draw the schematic symbols for various kinds of transformers. III

Explain the no-load condition of a transformer. II

Analyze the polarity of a transformer's windings. IV

Define *turns and voltage ratios* and *turns and current ratios,* and solve a proportion. III

Calculate transformer voltages. II

Describe current and voltage relationships. II

Calculate power in a transformer, and explain copper, eddy current, and hysteresis loss. II

Explain transformer efficiency, and name transformer ratings. II

Define *transformer impedance relationships,* and solve an impedance matching problem. III

Explain the function of an auto-transformer. II

04-015-210 **Discuss the uses of a power supply. III**

Define the functions of a rectifier, and diagram a half-wave rectifier and a full-wave rectifier. III

Define *ripple frequency.* I

Diagram a choke-input filter, a capacitor-input filter, and a pi filter. III

04-015-215   Solve circuit problems by trigonometry.   III

Define the trigonometric functions *sine, cosine,* and *tangent.*   I

Solve vectors by graphical analysis and by the Pythagorean theorem.   III

Define *rectangular coordinates* and *polar coordinates.*   I

Calculate impedance, using rectangular and polar coordinates.   II

04-015-220   Analyze a series RL circuit and a series RC circuit by varying frequency, resistance, applied voltage, and inductance.   IV

Determine the effects of frequency on *RL* circuits.   IV

Define the terms *cutoff* and *half-power point,* and determine the cutoff frequency of an *RL* circuit.   IV

Define *RL low-pass filter* and *RL high-pass filter.*   I

Solve vector diagrams for series *RC* circuits.   III

Determine the effects of frequency on *RC* circuits.   IV

Define *RC low-pass filter* and *RC high-pass filter.*   I

Solve for impedance in a series *RLC* circuit.   III

Define the *figure of merit* (Q) for a coil, *skin effect,* and *proximity effect.*   I

04-015-225   Analyze circuit behavior above and below the resonant frequency.   IV

Define the conditions for series resonance, and derive the expression for the resonant frequency.   III

Explain and calculate voltage gain across the reactive elements at resonance.   II

Diagram current and impedance curves at the resonant frequency. IV

Define bandwidth, and explain the effects of Q on bandwidth. II

Explain how series resonant circuits may be employed as filters. II

04-015-230 Analyze a parallel RL circuit by varying frequency, resistance, applied voltage, and inductance. IV

Calculate current, impedance, power, and power factor in a parallel *RL* circuit. II

Calculate current, impedance, power, and power factor in a parallel *RC* circuit. II

Compute current, impedance, power, and power factor in an *RLC* circuit. II

Analyze an ideal parallel *LC* circuit. IV

Describe a tank circuit. II

List the conditions for parallel resonance. I

Diagram current and impedance curves at the resonant frequency. III

Analyze a practical tank circuit. IV

Describe how parallel resonant circuits may be employed as filters. II

Explain when the effective resistance of the coil in an *RL* circuit must be considered. II

Calculate figure of merit, impedance, and current in a practical *RL* circuit. II

04-015-235 **Relate evidence and experiments to the concepts of quantum systems and quantum mechanics. IV**

Describe the Franck–Hertz experiment and its significance in predicting photon spectra that should arise when an atom changes its energy state. II

Given an energy-level diagram for an atom of mercury, predict the spectral lines that appear when the atom is bombarded with electrons. III

Describe the numerical results for the energy levels of atomic hydrogen. Include a comparison of the basic results of Balmer and Rydberg. II

Using Newton's law ($F = ma$) and the de Broglie hypothesis ($\lambda = h/mv$), find the energy-level relationship for atomic hydrogen. Relate the derivation to the wave mechanics of a "particle in a box." IV

Explain how Franck and Hertz's electron bombardment experiment revealed the presence of atomic energy levels. II

List reasons why the wave properties of atoms might be a possible explanation for discrete energy levels. II

Identify the four "quantum numbers" of an electron, and explain how they, with the help of the exclusion principle, make it possible to determine the electron configuration in any atom. II

Identify examples of the contributions of Heisenberg, Franck, Hertz, Pauli, de Broglie, Planck, and Schrödinger to the field of quantum physics. I

04-015-240 **Write and present a paper on an area in which physics is currently being widely employed and in which its frontiers are being expanded. Include a discussion of prospects for future development. III**

List laws from physics that are being widely used in research and industry. I

Find information about the work being done in an area of physics today. III

Describe the research being conducted in an industrial plant or in a research organization in your section of the country.   II

Describe the energy needs of modern society, and predict the potential of solar, atomic, and petroleum-derived power to meet those needs.   III

04-015-245   **Combine concepts, principles, and generalizations by producing an electric motor or transformer, wiring a model. Explain the model in terms of watts, voltage, resistance, kilowatt-hours, and electron movement.   V**

Given a description or diagram of a circuit and using the term *open circuit* or *closed circuit,* describe the circuit and tell whether the circuit is on or off.   II

Name the electrical component represented by a given symbol and tell one function of the component: battery or cells, switch, or resistance.   I

Demonstrate series circuits and parallel circuits by using the appropriate equipment and explaining the demonstration.   III

Match a given definition with one of the following terms: *volt, ampere, ohm, watt.*   I

Given Ohm's law (amperage = voltage/resistance) and values for two of the variables, solve for the third variable.   III

Find the kilowatt-hours used when given the time and the amount of electrical power consumed.   III

Given a description of the change of one form of energy into electrical energy, describe the original form of energy as chemical, mechanical, light, or heat energy.   II

Given a description of the results of an experiment designed to determine the electrical conductivity of a material such as paper, water, or copper, classify the material as a conductor or a nonconductor (insulator).   II

Explain the behavior of conductors, insulators, and semiconductors in terms of electron movement, and be able to give examples of each. II

Given a diagram of a dry cell or a voltaic cell, recognize the parts and their functions. Explain the flow of electricity through the cell and in a circuit. II

Match each of the following electronic components with its symbol, and explain the function of each component: diode, triode, capacitor, resistor, transistor, coil. II

Given examples of objects that produce current electricity, recognize the method used to produce electricity as magnetic or chemical. II

Locate and identify the parts (core, coil, source) of an electromagnet, given a description or diagram of one. I

04-015-250 **Predict possible uses for computers, and explain your predictions in as much detail as possible. III**

Define the following terms with reference to computers: *program, data, bit, memory, printout, card, nanosecond, binary, analog, digital, disc.* I

Demonstrate how numbers written in base ten can be stored in computers as base-two (binary) units. III

Describe the three main parts of a computer: input, central processor (control unit, arithmetic unit, and memory unit), output. II

Explain how computers have been used in at least two of the following areas: government, police work, education, transportation, space exploration, communications, business, cybernetics. II

Discuss the use of computers in modern society in relation to the ways in which the computer might advance or impede personal freedom. III

04-015-255 **Combine concepts, principles, and generalizations by developing mathematical functions to express relationships in physics and applying the equations in solving word problems. V**

Write an equation for a given mathematical relationship, and apply the equation in solving word problems. III

Solve word problems in vector addition and multiplication of a vector by a scalar (an ordinary number), using three methods: graph, components, trigonometry. III

Chemistry

04-020-005 **Given a measure of length, volume, or weight in any metric unit, convert the measure to any other metric unit of length, volume, or weight. II**

Identify the basic metric unit that is used for measuring each of the following: length, weight, volume, temperature. I

Define each of the prefixes used to indicate different units of measure in the metric system: *milli-, centi-, deci-, kilo-*. I

04-020-010 **Show that you can perform the measurements required in laboratory experiments. III**

Measure the length of objects in metric units to within 0.1 centimeter. II

Measure the volume of solids and liquids in metric units to within 1 milliliter. II

Calculate the volume of rectangular solids to within 0.1 cubic centimeter. II

Measure the weight of objects in metric units to within 0.1 gram. II

Measure temperatures to within 1° C or 1° F. II

04-020-015 **Use laboratory apparatus safely and correctly. III**

Locate on a diagram the following parts of a laboratory gas burner: barrel, collar, air inlet, gas inlet, gas valve, and base. Identify the function of each of these parts, and describe the correct technique for operating a laboratory gas burner. I

Identify basic types of laboratory glassware, and describe how each is used. II

Demonstrate safe glasscleaning techniques. III

Demonstrate techniques of preparing glass tubing for use in setting up experimental apparatus. III

04-020-020 **Draw or build models showing the structure of matter (atoms, elements, compounds, isotopes, etc.). III**

Given illustrations, samples, or models, identify each as an element, an atom, a compound, or a mixture. II

Given a drawing, identify the basic parts of an atom. I

Given a model or formula for a molecule, identify the number of atoms and elements in the molecule represented. I

Given a model representing a molecule of a compound, select the formula that matches the model. I

Given atomic models of isotopes of the same element, identify the parts and tell how the models differ. II

04-020-025 **Identify the phases of matter, discuss changes at the molecular level, and describe the properties at each phase. III**

Given a property of matter, define the property and classify it into one of the following groups: general properties, specific properties, physical properties, chemical properties. II

Demonstrate one way to show that matter takes up space. III

Demonstrate one way to show that matter has weight. III

Differentiate between weight and mass. III

Recognize several properties of an object or a substance, including color, shape, size, texture, taste, odor, and state of matter. Recognize the sense used to determine each of these properties. II

Explain how plasma differs from solids, liquids, and gases. Given a list of substances, recognize those that are plasma. II

Given a situation in which an object or substance must fit into a prescribed space or conform to a given weight capacity, explain whether it is more important to know about the material's weight or its volume.   II

Given a list of substances, identify each substance as a gas, a liquid, or a solid.   I

Describe a solid, a liquid, and a gas in terms of definite or indefinite volume and shape.   II

Explain the relative motion of the molecules and the relative distances between the molecules in the solid, liquid, and gaseous phases of matter.   II

Identify the points of phase change, and describe the processes involved: boiling, boiling point, freezing, freezing point, melting, melting point, sublimation, condensation, vaporization.   II

04-020-030   **Perceive relationships expressed in the kinetic theory of gases, and solve problems utilizing this theory.   IV**

Solve word problems concerning the amount of heat energy in given bodies at various temperatures and problems concerning the exchange of heat between various bodies.   III

Use the kinetic theory of matter to describe molecular motion of the different phases of matter.   III

Describe the relationship between the molecular theory of gases and Boyle's law. Solve word problems, using Boyle's law.   III

Describe the relationship between the ideal gas law and the kinetic theory of gases. Solve word problems, using the ideal gas law.   III

Find the amount of positive or negative work done by a gas that is expanding or contracting relative to its surroundings during adiabatic and isothermal processes.   III

Using Bernoulli's law, solve word problems and answer questions concerning moving fluids. III

04-020-035 **Demonstrate the effects of heat on matter, describing the effects in terms of molecular change. III**

Read a thermometer to the nearest degree in either °F or °C. II

Identify the boiling and freezing points of water on both the Fahrenheit scale and the centigrade scale. I

Demonstrate the boiling points of various water solutions. III

Using the terms *expand* or *contract,* describe the state to which matter changes when heat energy is added or taken away. II

Given two states of matter, tell whether heat must be added or taken away to transform the first into the second state. Name the process involved. I

Given a description or illustration of a change of state of a liquid, explain whether the temperature of the substance was at the freezing point or the boiling point. II

Conduct an experiment to demonstrate the cause-and-effect relationship between temperature and the time it takes for a substance to dissolve in water. Use the following steps. III
1. Hypothesis (guess of results based on previous observation and knowledge)
2. Design (steps you will take, material you will use)
3. Record of observations
4. Conclusions

Describe how heat affects the amount of solid substance that will dissolve in water. II

Given two states of matter, explain what occurs when heat is added or taken away. Explain what has happened to the molecules between the first and second state, and give the name of the process. II

Given a substance, explain the effect of heat on the volume of the substance and on the speed of the molecular action or motion. II

Explain the difference between the scientific definitions of *heat* and *temperature.* Use these terms in a sentence. II

Define *conduction, convection,* and *radiation.* I

Explain the operation of the following devices in response to temperature changes: thermostat, thermometer, thermocouple. II

04-020-040 **Construct a model of an element to show the relationship between the atomic number of the element and the number of electrons in an atom of the element. III**

Recognize the relationship between the atomic number of an element and the number of electrons in the atom of the element. II

Given atomic models of isotopes of the same element, identify the parts and tell how the models differ. I

04-020-045 **Given a description or a diagram, discuss atoms, elements, molecules, compounds, and mixtures. III**

Given illustrations or models of different substances, identify the substance illustrated as an element, an atom, a compound, or a mixture. I

From a given definition or description of a substance, recognize the substance as a compound or a mixture. II

Given a model representing a molecule of a compound, select the formula that matches the model. I

Define the terms *matter, molecule, atom, electron,* and *neutron.* I

Given a list of early theories on matter, match each theory with the scientist who furthered it: Dalton, Boyle, Democritus, Empedocles. I

Interpret information obtained from simple experimental tests to identify elements. II

Explain the difference between an atom and a molecule, given a diagram, drawing, or description of each. II

Given a model or formula for a molecule, determine the number of atoms and elements in the molecule represented. III

Classify common substances as elements or compounds, given symbols, formulas, or models. II

Classify substances (e.g., sugar, salt, glass) as crystalline or noncrystalline, given a description or drawing of the molecular arrangements. II

04-020-050 Use the periodic table to predict the chemical and physical properties of elements, basing your prediction on a knowledge of their atomic numbers. III

Locate the following families of elements on a periodic table: inert gases (noble gases), metals (sodium family), calcium family, transitional elements, nitrogen family, oxygen family, halogen family. I

Using the periodic table horizontally and vertically, show your understanding of physical changes and chemical reactivity within a family, within a period, family to family, and period to period. II

Given a brief description of an atomic theory, match the theory with the scientist (Dalton, Thomson, Rutherford, Bohr, Schrödinger, Einstein, de Broglie) who advanced the theory. I

Given information about a particular element from the periodic chart, recognize the electron configuration that represents an atom of that element. II

04-020-055 **Given ionic equations that represent the reactions of selected acids or bases, predict the properties of the substances and their reactions to different indicators. III**

Recognize given properties as characteristics of acids, bases, or both. II

Given the behavior of an indicator in the pH scale, tell whether a particular color indicates an acidic solution or a basic solution. I

Balance given ionic equations or empirical equations that represent the reactions of acids and/or bases. II

04-020-060 **Given a list of elements (including both metals and non-metals), predict which elements will form chemical bonds with one another and whether these compounds are ionic or covalent. III**

Name the conditions that are necessary for atoms to form chemical bonds (ionic and covalent). I

Given elements that react to form ionic compounds and using the periodic chart, write empirical formulas for the compounds. III

Given elements that react to form covalent molecules, use the periodic table to write molecular formulas for the molecules. III

04-020-065 **Demonstrate your ability to combine concepts, principles, and generalizations by designing an experiment that will demonstrate the differential behaviors of solutions that have the same molar strength but contain either ionic or nonionic solutes. V**

Given the weight in grams of a sample of a substance and using a chart or table of atomic weights, calculate the maximum amount of a 1-M aqueous solution that can be prepared. II

Given a description of an experiment in which a substance has been tested for its electrolytic properties, interpret the results of the experiment according to the Ionic Theory of Conductivity. II

Given the empirical formulas of substances that conduct electricity in a water solution, write ionic equations to represent what happens when these substances dissociate. III

Demonstrate the differences between the behavior of solutions (such as salt water) and pure substances (such as water) according to time required to reach boiling and freezing points, respective temperatures at which boiling and freezing take place, and respective vapor pressures. III

As freezing or boiling of a solution continues, predict how the properties of the solution (vapor pressure, concentration of solute, density, boiling temperature, freezing temperature) will vary. Test your predictions. III

04-020-070 **Perceive the relationship of nuclear equations to the decay of two isotopes (such as 131_1 and 32_p). Determine the relative number of particles emitted by each nucleus after a given time period.   IV**

Apply the concept of half-life of radioactive isotopes to solve word problems.   III

Given a nuclear reaction with all the reactants and prodducts described except one, complete the equation for the reaction. Classify the type of reaction as alpha or beta decay, fusion, or fission.   II

Describe fusion and fission reactions.   II

04-020-075 **Present a report analyzing the use of hydrocarbons in industry and some associated problems.   IV**

Describe the processes of fractional distillation, polymerization, and cracking. Recognize illustrations of each process.   II

Given examples of chemical reactions involving aromatic hydrocarbons, classify the reaction as halogenation, nitration, sulfonation, or Friedel-Crafts.   II

Investigate the problems associated with the use of hydrocarbons and the possibility of their effect on ozone.   III

04-020-080   **Knowing the value of K_A of an acid and its concentration in a solution, calculate the pH of the solution.   III**

Given the equation for the reaction of an acid and a base and a table of values for K_A, explain whether reactants or products are favored.   II

Given the volume and concentration of a strong acid and a strong base, calculate the hydrogen-ion and hydroxide-ion concentration for the acid–base solution.   II

04-020-085   **In an experiment involving a chemical change in which one of the products is a gas, predict the weight and volume of gas. Compare your prediction with the actual yield.   IV**

Given the formula of a compound and the atomic weights of its elements, calculate the percentage composition of the compound.   II

Given the percentage composition of a compound and the atomic weights of its elements, calculate the empirical formula of the compound.   II

Given the volume of one mole of a gas at standard temperature and pressure (STP) and the density of the gas at STP, calculate the gram–molecular weight of the gas.   II

Given a balanced equation and the atomic weights of the elements involved, calculate the weight of a reactant required to produce a known amount of a product or the weight of a product produced by a known amount of a reactant.   II

Given the volume per mole of a gas, calculate the mass needed to produce a given volume of the gas (at STP) or the volume of the gas produced by a given mass.   II

Given a balanced equation of reacting gases at STP, calculate the volume of a reactant (or product) when the volume of a product (or reactant) is known. III

04-020-090 **Combine concepts, principles, and generalizations by designing an experiment that demonstrates chemical change, and explain the chemical changes that take place. V**

Design, set up, and perform an experiment that will demonstrate the 2:1 ratio of hydrogen to oxygen in water. V

Describe two processes to make an impure water supply potable. III

Describe how hard water can be made soft, and list the advantages and disadvantages of soft water. III

Given a description of the process of soap making, bleaching, or fermentation, explain the function of the ingredients. Describe the products that result from each process. II

Given a description of a fire that involves any of the following combustible materials, identify what method(s) should be used and what method(s) should not be used to extinguish the fire: wood, electrical wiring, oil, fat, cloth. I

Set up and conduct an experiment to demonstrate the removal of tarnish on silver objects. III

Tell what first-aid measures should be taken when a specified poisonous substance is swallowed. I

04-020-095 **Combine concepts, principles, and generalizations by developing a scheme of analysis for identifying the composition of an unknown solution or solid. Use a variety of laboratory tests, flame tests, precipitation, borax bead test, blowpipe tests (cobalt nitrate tests), and paper chromatography. Identify the unknown. V**

Perform chemical tests on several known solutions or solids and one unknown solution or solid to identify their composition. III

Given a scheme of analysis, determine the composition of an unknown solution or solid.   IV

04-020-100   Using the table of oxidation potentials, predict the reaction of three pairs of substances with one another, and explain the bases for your predictions.   III

Explain the difference between oxidation and reduction in terms of experimental chemical behavior, change in oxidation number, and half-reaction equations.   II

Given the reactants of an electrolytic process, go through the following procedures.   III
1. Write half-cell equations for those substances oxidized and tell why oxidation has occurred.
2. Write half-cell equations for the substances reduced and tell why reduction has occurred.
3. Write the products and balance the equation.

Given a redox equation, go through the following procedures.   III
1. Demonstrate how conservation of charge and matter is maintained, using half-reactions.
2. Balance the equation.
3. Use the table of oxidation potentials (E^0) to predict whether or not the reaction will take place spontaneously.
4. Compute the E^0 total for the redox reactions.

Write half-cell equations to describe desirable and undesirable redox reactions.   III

Explain how Faraday's experiments in electrochemistry gave further evidence for Dalton's atomic theory.   II

04-020-105   Design an experiment in which you have to demonstrate how different forms of energy (including heat energy) can be produced in a chemical reaction.   V

Given the equations for endothermic or exothermic reactions and a table of heats of reaction between elements, calculate the amount of heat lost or gained in forming the product.   II

Describe the relationship between chemical and mechanical forms of energy. II

Explain how the Law of Conservation of Energy applies to the production of energy in chemical reactions. II

Describe the difference in the relative amounts of energy involved in a physical change, a chemical change, and a nuclear change. II

04-020-110   Perceive the difference between energy changes associated with chemical reactions and energy changes associated with physical changes.   IV

Given equations for chemical reactions, explain whether the reactions are endothermic or exothermic. II

Classify described substances as elements, compounds, or mixtures. II

Describe phase changes associated with the gain or loss of energy. II

04-020-115   Discuss the gas laws in terms of the amount of kinetic energy possessed by the molecules of gaseous substances.   III

Express the relationship between the volume and the pressure of a confined gas, and solve related problems. II

Express the relationship between the volume of a confined gas and its absolute temperature, and solve related problems. II

Given Avogadro's number, the periodic table, and the mass of a given gas, calculate the number of moles and molecules contained in that gas. II

Interpret a graph that illustrates changes in the amount of kinetic energy possessed by the molecules of a gaseous substance at different temperatures. II

04-020-120   Predict how changes in pressure, temperature, concentration of reactants, and addition of a catalyst would affect the rate of a reaction and the point of equilibrium for that reaction.   III

Given the nature of reactants, the concentration of reactants, the temperature change, and the addition of a catalyst, describe how each condition affects the rate of a chemical reaction.   II

Given a closed equilibrium system, predict how the system would shift because of changes in pressure, temperature, or concentration.   III

Given two solutions of known molarity and a table of solubility products, predict whether a precipitate will form when two solutions are mixed.   III

Given an equilibrium system, describe how the heat content and the random distribution of the reactants and products vary.   II

04-020-125   Given reactants and conditions for several organic reactions, predict the principal products and identify these products by formula and name.   III

Given a random list of chemical properties, identify the properties that are characteristic of organic compounds.   I

Given the names and the structural and molecular formulas of organic compounds, classify the compounds as saturated, unsaturated, or aromatic hydrocarbons.   II

Given the structural formula of an organic compound, classify the compound according to the functional group (alcohol, aldehyde, carboxyl, amine, carbonyl), and name the compound.   II

Given the reactants and conditions of an organic reaction, recognize principal products and balance the equation.   II

04-020-130 **Discuss how the chemical and physical characteristics of carbohydrates and lipids, proteins, and nucleic acids make them particularly well suited as sources of energy, enzymes, and hereditary material in the living cell. III**

Recognize a simple sugar, a starch, a lipid, and a protein, given the structural formula and chemical characteristics for each form. II

Given the building materials and energy sources available to the cell, predict changes in cell metabolism. III

Given the properties (composition, acid-base characteristics, structure) of enzymes, explain how the enzymes catalyze chemical reactions in the cell. II

Given the chemical makeup of hereditary material, describe its role in protein synthesis, its method of production, and mechanisms of its transmission from one generation to another. II

04-020-135 **Discuss relationships of properties of colloidal particles to properties of macromolecules, such as proteins, that are of colloidal size. II**

Recognize the chemical and physical properties of colloids that account for the behavior and practical application of colloids. II

In living things, recognize particles of colloidal size. II

04-020-140 **Design an experiment, formulate a hypothesis, record your procedures and observations, draw conclusions regarding the hypothesis, and report your results. V**

Design and perform an experiment concerning a problem in chemistry that you have defined. Write a complete laboratory report that demonstrates your ability to combine concepts, principles, and generalizations. V

Make an inference from a set of observations drawn from chemistry. IV

From a list of observations drawn from chemistry, recognize the observations that support a given inference. II

Recognize observations and inferences from a mixed list of these drawn from chemistry. II

Represent chemical data in a table and a graph. II

Translate chemical data from a graph into a table. II

From a list of statements, recognize statements that appear to originate from a graph about chemistry. II

Explain the way two variables and a graph of chemical data are related. II

Given a list of safety rules and information about laboratory techniques in wearing safety equipment, locating and using fire extinguishers, using a first-aid kit, handling chemicals, mixing acid solutions, and cleaning up, demonstrate that you can apply the rules and information during your investigations and experiments and that you understand their purposes. III

04-020-145 **Given a description of a scientific experiment, organize the information given into a complete laboratory report that includes title, problem, hypothesis, procedure, data, and conclusion. V**

Given a scientific event or situation, write questions that, when answered, help to explain the event or situation. III

Given a question, the answer to which would help explain a scientific event or situation, select sources of information or activities that may lead to an answer to the question. I

Given a possible answer to a scientific question, write a testable hypothesis that may provide an answer to the questions. V

Given a testable hypothesis, design a laboratory procedure (experiment) that will test the hypothesis. V

Given the results of a laboratory procedure (experimental), record them and display them in the form of a table and a graph.   III

Given a table or graph of the results of an experiment, interpret the results, make inferences and predictions based upon the results, and determine whether the results support, refute, or have no bearing upon the hypothesis tested.   IV

Appendix

Biology

04-005-005   Support or reject, using the experimental designs of Stanley Miller and Sidney Fox, the heterotroph hypothesis regarding a possible sequence of events that might have produced the first polypeptides.   VI

04-005-010   Differentiate between theories that explain the geologic record of life in the past and those explaining the origin of life.   IV

04-005-015   Compare examples of straightline, divergent, and convergent evolution.   VI

04-005-020   Given an example of evidence for the theory of evolution and an interpretation of that evidence, determine whether this interpretation supports Darwin's theory of natural selection or Lamarck's theory of inheritance of acquired characteristics.   IV

04-005-025   Describe the characteristics and functions of plant and animal cells.   III

04-005-030   Compare prokaryotic and eukaryotic cells on the basis of size and compartmentalization, and recognize examples of each type of cell.   IV

04-005-035   Analyze the process of diffusion by diagram, description, or other means.   IV

04-005-040   Discuss three reasons why man has devised and used schemes of classification since early recorded history.   III

04-005-045   Use a taxonomic key to classify three given animals and three given plants. Describe each step you used, and end with the scientific name of each animal.   III

04-005-050   Describe and draw structures of organisms that illustrate diversity among the lower animal phyla.   IV

04-005-055   Describe and illustrate examples of diversity among the higher animal phyla, and explain the significance of these differences.   IV

04-005-060   Through diagrams, pictures, or models, demonstrate the adaptive powers of plants and animals.   III

04-005-065   Describe adaptations of muscular and skeletal systems of three selected vertebrates and three selected invertebrates that aid each organism in obtaining food.   II

04-005-070   Using a specific plant and animal, develop an experiment that shows the mechanism by which each obtains and produces energy and synthesizes organic compounds.   V

04-005-075   Describe the structural components of vascular plants.   II

04-005-080   Given a vascular plant and a nonvascular plant, describe the intake of nutrients and production of waste products, identifying the structures involved in each process.   III

04-005-085   Determine environmental factors affecting photosynthesis, and describe experiments that test whether light is necessary for photosynthesis, whether CO_2 is necessary for photosynthesis, and whether chlorophyll is necessary for photosynthesis.   IV

04-005-090   Support the statement "Species survival is dependent upon efficient complementarity of structure and function."   IV

04-005-095   Develop a hypothesis that explains how multicellularity might bring about a higher behavioral level in multicellular forms.   V

04-005-100   Compare and contrast the circulatory and respiratory systems in three types of higher animals.   IV

04-005-105   Discuss the gathering, digestion, and utilization of food in animals, and evaluate the efficiency of specific animals in carrying out these processes.   VI

04-005-110   Describe the excretory system and explain the need for a proper tissue-fluid balance within an organism.   III

04-005-115   Describe the operation of the components of a homeo-static system, and analyze the importance of homeo-stasis.   IV

04-005-120   Analyze the manner in which hormones function as regulatory substances within the endocrine systems of vertebrates.   IV

04-005-125   Discuss the relationship among the parts of the human nervous system.   IV

04-005-130   Perceive the relationship of the behavior of a person who is threatened and then struck by an object and the resultant behavioral changes in the endocrine and nervous systems. Emphasize the interrelatedness of the activities of these systems.   IV

04-005-135   Through research, investigate the process by which DNA was discovered and its molecular structure determined.   III

04-005-140   Discuss the characteristics of seeds and the conditions required for plant growth.   III

04-005-145   Discuss the systems of the human body—digestive, circulatory, respiratory, nervous, reproductive, glandular, excretory, skeletal, muscular, and integumentary—with respect to the important general functions of each system.   III

04-005-150   Define the term *disease* and relate it to microorganisms.   IV

04-005-155   Investigate the characteristics of given organisms that are harmful to man, and explain means of controlling these organisms.   III

04-005-160   On the basis of your knowledge of the effect of environmental factors on the growth of microorganisms, discuss factors that make a microorganism infectious or non-infectious to a particular host.   III

04-005-165   Collect information about and discuss four types of human diseases.   III

04-005-170   Compare reasons that people who drink alcoholic beverages give to justify their actions with reasons given by drug users to justify their use of drugs.   IV

04-005-175   Discuss the human reproductive system and describe present-day mores related to reproduction.   III

04-005-180   Compare and contrast the reproductive process in plants, insects, and animals.   IV

04-005-185   Use specific examples drawn from the plant and animal kingdom to show your understanding of ways the differences in the mechanisms of mitosis and meiosis affect the offspring that result from asexual or sexual reproduction.   III

04-005-190   Compare and contrast the appearance of fish, bird, and pig embryos at comparable stages of development, and indicate the significance of the similarities and differences.   IV

04-005-195   Compare the processes of mitosis and meiosis on the following bases: desired outcome in terms of chromosome number, number of cells produced, fate of cells produced, site of occurrence in man.   IV

04-005-200   Given the genotype of an individual, determine all the possible gene combinations in the gametes that can be formed by that plant or animal.   IV

04-005-205   Combine concepts, principles, and generalizations by designing an experiment with fruit flies to illustrate Mendel's laws. Complete each stage of the experiment, and evaluate your results.   V

04-005-210   Discuss examples of sex-limited inheritance.   III

04-005-215   Draw and analyze your family tree or the family tree of an acquaintance. Attempt to explain the presence of three family traits according to Mendel's laws and according to present-day knowledge of genetics, citing the scientist responsible for theories you use.   IV

04-005-220   Compare innate behavior to learned behavior.   IV

04-005-225   Use correct terminology to describe learned and unlearned behavior in a group of selected animals observed
for several hours.   III

04-005-230   Combine concepts, principles, and generalizations by
designing an experiment in which the following principles of learning are demonstrated: learned and unlearned
behavior, memorization, forgetting, and relearning.
Include these procedures in the experiments.   V
1. Formulate a hypothesis based on observations.
2. Organize your experiment with variables.
3. Draw conclusions and make generalizations.
4. Write a formal report of your findings.

04-005-235   Trace the flow of energy from the sun, through the living
system, and back into the abiotic environment.   III

04-005-240   Construct and analyze a food web based on a given
chart of a biomass pyramid.   IV

04-005-245   Relate marine biotic forms to their abiotic environment
by describing environmental conditions found in the
spray, intertidal, and subtidal zones, and give examples
of the types of marine organisms that could best survive
in each zone.   IV

04-005-250   Analyze four processes that are related to most patterns
of ecological succession.   IV

04-005-255   Analyze a problem related to pollution, and suggest a
solution.   IV

04-005-260   Draw conclusions about the effect that man's ability to
control his environment has on other living things.
Include at least three examples of control and the means
used to apply it.   IV

04-005-265   Given the continuation of the expansion of cities and
the destruction of natural life, predict the changes that
may occur in the total environment. Report evidence to
support your predictions.   III

04-005-270   Compare human and animal population growth curves.
IV

04-005-275 Given a scientific question or problem involving biology, combine concepts, principles, and generalizations by developing relevant hypotheses that can be tested through a series of experiments. V

04-005-280 Analyze statistics, tables, and charts, and use the information to interpret biological data. IV

04-005-285 Discuss the total magnification of any combination of objective and eyepiece powers on a microscope with respect to specimens to be studied. III

04-005-290 Combine concepts, principles, and generalizations by designing an investigation of a biological problem that involves the use of the microscope and other tools of the modern biologist. V

04-005-295 Demonstrate your familiarity with medical terminology related to the body systems, including disorders. III

Earth Science

04-010-005   Show that you can determine locations of areas represented on maps and use topographic information accurately.   IV

04-010-010   Discuss the relative positions of the various astronomical bodies in the universe. Describe the nature of forces among the astronomical bodies.   III

04-010-015   Describe the planet Earth in relation to the solar system, and discuss ways in which it is typical or atypical.   III

04-010-020   Present the problems related to space travel, based on information gained from manned and unmanned space-flights.   III

04-010-025   Determine the relationship of our galaxy to other galaxies.   IV

04-010-030   Determine the mode of origin of specific rock types.   IV

04-010-035   Discuss the rock cycle in terms of the processes that act on the earth materials and the products that result.   III

04-010-040   Relate a mineral's properties to its atomic structure.   IV

04-010-045   Discuss the composition of Earth, conditions under which various materials were formed, and the mechanisms for tectonic change.   III

04-010-050   Identify changes that occur in the features of Earth, and relate the causes of these changes to the results.   IV

04-010-055   Perceive relationships of the various factors that create weather conditions.   IV

04-010-060   Show your understanding of the observational data used by meteorologists in predicting weather.   II

04-010-065   Apply a knowledge of the characteristics of fronts to make weather predictions, including these weather elements: temperature, barometric pressure, cloud cover, precipitation, wind velocity.   III

04-010-070   Discuss the relationships between changes in temperature and pressure, and changes in solar heating with respect to their effect on weather conditions.   III

04-010-075   Show your understanding of hydrology by predicting the availability of water in particular areas.   III

04-010-080   Show your understanding of the nature of the sea–air interface.   II

04-010-085   Given an erosional agent (water, wind, ice), relate the effects of gravity and kinetic energy to the erosion of different types of material.   IV

04-010-090   Using descriptions of environments, biome maps, and climatogram information, determine the probable distribution of living things in a given environment.   IV

04-010-095   Predict the success of various methods of preventing and controlling pollution.   III

04-010-100   Discuss the work done by a group of scientists on sediment dating and radioactive-clock methods of dating. Analyze how their results clarify the mechanisms involved in the decline of one group of animals and the increase in another group of animals.   IV

04-010-105   Demonstrate your ability to perceive relationships in a laboratory experiment by making inferences and predictions based upon quantitative results that you have tabulated and graphed.   IV

04-010-110   Make predictions based on your analysis of laboratory observations and measurements stated in a table or in graph form, using either interpolation or extrapolation. (Interpolation: predicting between two points; extrapolation: predicting beyond the last known point.)   IV

04-010-115   Combine concepts, principles, and generalizations by designing and conducting an experiment to test the validity of a given hypothesis and by analyzing and reporting the results.   V

Physics

04-015-005   Given a brief history of the development of a physical law, discuss the law's history by indicating the period of time that the law was first a hypothesis, the period that the hypothesis became a theory, and the period that the theory was recognized as a law.   III

04-015-010   Explain   physical   and   chemical   properties   and changes.   II

04-015-015   Make measurements and calculations with respect to time, distance, area, and volume as required in word problems and express results in scientific notation.   III

04-015-020   Use the metric system of measurement by applying the system in all scientific experiments performed during the year.   IV

04-015-025   Discuss the relative positions of stationary and moving objects.   III

04-015-030   Identify the phases of matter, discuss the changes at the molecular level, and describe the properties at each phase.   III

04-015-035   Discuss the relationships between mass, volume, and density.   III

04-015-040   Given a discription or a diagram, discuss atoms, elements, molecules, compounds, and mixtures.   III

04-015-045   Construct a model of an element to show the relationship between the atomic number of the element and the number of electrons in an atom of the element.   III

04-015-050   Given a demonstration of a moving object, use these terms to explain the phenomena: *force, inertia, energy, work, friction.*   III

04-015-055   Combine concepts, principles, and generalizations by developing relationships among the various properties of objects moving in space.   V

04-015-060   Combine concepts, principles, and generalizations by designing three experiments that show the increase or decrease of the speed of an object and velocity as a function of time. V

04-015-065   Demonstrate the properties of force and the ways in which properties interact. III

04-015-070   Given a simple machine, demonstrate its mechanical advantages and devise a simple tool of your own. V

04-015-075   Combine concepts, principles, and generalizations about Newton's basic laws by designing a simple experiment that illustrates their application. Develop a hypothesis, test it with variables, draw conclusions, and make generalizations. V

04-015-080   Analyze the relationships expressed in the conservation laws, and solve problems utilizing these laws. IV

04-015-085   Explain the processes by which nuclear energy is produced, and evaluate the benefits in relation to the possible negative effects. VI

04-015-090   Demonstrate the effects of heat on matter. Describe the effects in terms of molecular change. III

04-015-095   Interpret diagrams that illustrate the principles of sound. III

04-015-100   Demonstrate the characteristics of wave motion. III

04-015-105   Combine concepts, principles, and generalizations by designing and presenting a demonstration of the nature and behavior of light. V

04-015-110   Make judgments that involve the characteristics of light waves. VI

04-015-115   Analyze the relationships expressed in the quantum theory of light by solving problems utilizing this theory. IV

04-015-120   Present the evidence for modern theories concerning wavelike properties of particles of matter. III

04-015-125 Analyze the relationships expressed in the kinetic theory of gases and solve problems utilizing this theory. IV

04-015-130 Describe the internal-combustion engine in terms of potential, kinetic, electrical, chemical, and mechanical energy. II

04-015-135 Analyze the relationships between electric charges and electric current under various conditions. IV

04-015-140 List the components of an electric circuit, and compare them with those of a simple hydraulic system. IV

04-015-145 Discuss two kinds of potential difference, voltage rise and voltage drop, and describe the symbols used to differentiate them. III

04-015-150 Connect an ohmmeter in a circuit to make resistance measurements. III

04-015-155 Discuss the relation between voltage drop across a resister and the ohmic value of its resistance. III

04-015-160 Demonstrate that varying the resistance affects current in a series circuit in which the voltage is held constant. III

04-015-165 Use variational analysis as a tool in understanding how circuit quantities interact. III

04-015-170 Determine quantities in a complex circuit by applying basic theories of electricity. IV

04-015-175 Discuss the relationship between electricity and magnetism. III

04-015-180 Analyze the relationships between magnetic fields and the currents producing them. IV

04-015-185 Demonstrate the principles of electromagnetic induction. III

04-015-190 List the physical factors in a capacitor that affect its capacitance, and derive an equation for capacitance from these physical factors. III

04-015-195 Discuss the uses of ac and dc power. III

04-015-200 Demonstrate the phase relationship between current and voltage in an inductive ac circuit. III

04-015-205 Determine the direction of induced voltage in the secondary conditions. IV

04-015-210 Discuss the uses of a power supply. III

04-015-215 Solve circuit problems by trigonometry. III

04-015-220 Analyze a series *RL* circuit and a series *RC* circuit by varying frequency, resistance, applied voltage, and inductance. IV

04-015-225 Analyze circuit behavior above and below the resonant frequency. IV

04-015-230 Analyze a parallel *RL* circuit by varying frequency, resistance, applied voltage, and inductance. IV

04-015-235 Relate evidence and experiments to the concepts of quantum systems and quantum mechanics. IV

04-015-240 Write and present a paper on an area in which physics is currently being widely employed and in which its frontiers are being expanded. Include a discussion of prospects for future development. III

04-015-245 Combine concepts, principles, and generalizations by producing an electric motor or transformer, wiring a model. Explain the model in terms of watts, voltage, resistance, kilowatt-hours; and electron movement. V

04-015-250 Predict possible uses for computers, and explain your predictions in as much detail as possible. III

04-015-255 Combine concepts, principles, and generalizations by developing mathematical functions to express relationships in physics and applying the equations in solving word problems. V

Chemistry

04-020-005   Given a measure of length, volume, or weight in any metric unit, convert the measure to any other metric unit of length, volume, or weight.   II

04-020-010   Show that you can perform the measurements required in laboratory experiments.   III

04-020-015   Use laboratory apparatus safely and correctly.   III

04-020-020   Draw or build models showing the structure of matter (atoms, elements, compounds, isotopes, etc.).   III

04-020-025   Identify the phases of matter, discuss changes at the molecular level, and describe the properties at each phase.   III

04-020-030   Perceive relationships expressed in the kinetic theory of gases, and solve problems utilizing this theory.   IV

04-020-035   Demonstrate the effects of heat on matter, describing the effects in terms of molecular change.   III

04-020-040   Construct a model of an element to show the relationship between the atomic number of the element and the number of electrons in an atom of the element.   III

04-020-045   Given a description or a diagram, discuss atoms, elements, molecules, compounds, and mixtures.   III

04-020-050   Use the periodic table to predict the chemical and physical properties of elements, basing your prediction on a knowledge of their atomic numbers.   III

04-020-055   Given ionic equations that represent the reactions of selected acids or bases, predict the properties of the substances and their reactions to different indicators.   III

04-020-060   Given a list of elements (including both metals and nonmetals), predict which elements will form chemical bonds with one another and whether these compounds are ionic or covalent.   III

04-020-065   Demonstrate your ability to combine concepts, principles, and generalizations by designing an experiment that will demonstrate the differential behaviors of solutions that have the same molar strength but contain either ionic or nonionic solutes.   V

04-020-070   Perceive the relationship of nuclear equations to the decay of two isotopes (such as 131_1 and 32_p). Determine the relative number of particles emitted by each nucleus after a given time period.   IV

04-020-075   Present a report analyzing the use of hydrocarbons in industry and some associated problems.   IV

04-020-080   Knowing the value of K_A of an acid and its concentration in a solution, calculate the pH of the solution.   III

04-020-085   In an experiment involving a chemical change in which one of the products is a gas, predict the weight and volume of gas. Compare your prediction with the actual yield.   IV

04-020-090   Combine concepts, principles, and generalizations by designing an experiment that demonstrates chemical change, and explain the chemical changes that take place.   V

04-020-095   Combine concepts, principles, and generalizations by developing a scheme of analysis for identifying the composition of an unknown solution or solid. Use a variety of laboratory tests, flame tests, precipitation, borax bead test, blowpipe tests (cobalt nitrate tests), and paper chromatography. Identify the unknown.   V

04-020-100   Using the table of oxidation potentials, predict the reaction of three pairs of substances with one another, and explain the bases for your predictions.   III

04-020-105   Design an experiment in which you have to demonstrate how different forms of energy (including heat energy) can be produced in a chemical reaction.   V

04-020-110   Perceive the difference between energy changes associated with chemical reactions and energy changes associated with physical changes.   IV

04-020-115   Discuss the gas laws in terms of the amount of kinetic energy possessed by the molecules of gaseous substances. III

04-020-120   Predict how changes in pressure, temperature, concentration of reactants, and addition of a catalyst would affect the rate of a reaction and the point of equilibrium for that reaction. III

04-020-125   Given reactants and conditions for several organic reactions, predict the principal products and identify these products by formula and name. III

04-020-130   Discuss how the chemical and physical characteristics of carbohydrates and lipids, proteins, and nucleic acids make them particularly well suited as sources of energy, enzymes, and hereditary material in the living cell. III

04-020-135   Discuss relationships of properties of colloidal particles to properties of macromolecules, such as proteins, that are of colloidal size. II

04-020-140   Design an experiment, formulate a hypothesis, record your procedures and observations, draw conclusions regarding the hypothesis, and report your results. V

04-020-145   Given a description of a scientific experiment, organize the information given into a complete laboratory report that includes title, problem, hypothesis, procedure, data, and conclusion. V

Index

References are to volumes, followed by the numbers of sections in the text. Volume abbreviations are LA (Language Arts), MA (Mathematics), SC (Science), SS (Social Science).

Graphs, charts, and tables (continued)
  parametric forms, MA-020-025
  shipping and mailing, MA-010-130
  See also Diagrams
Gravity, SC-010-010, 085; SC-015-050, 065, 075. See
    also Weight
Great Britain. See England
Greek influences
  democracy, SS-010-010
  drama, LA-025-015, 090
Gross national product, SS-005-100, 120
  components, SS-005-110
  price index, effect of, SS-005-105
Group behavior, SS-020-050, 055, 170; SS-025-080, 085
  conflicts, literature dealing with, LA-025-045, 135
  discussion groups, LA-005-095, 100, 105, 115
  power, exercise of, LA-005-110; SS-020-015
  prejudice, literature dealing with, LA-025-155
  racial discrimination (see Racial discrimination
      and conflict)
  social controls (see Social controls)
  special-interest groups, SS-010-175, 180
  types, SS-020-060
  See also Behavior; Minority and ethnic groups;
      Psychology
Guild system, SS-010-015
Guns, sale of, SS-010-170

Health
  diseases (see Diseases)
  insurance, SC-005-020
Heat
  exchange between various bodies, SC-015-125;
      SC-020-030
  matter, effect on, SC-015-090; SC-020-025, 035
  production through chemical reaction, SC-020-105
  solar heating, SC-010-070
  See also Temperature
Heavenly bodies. See Planets and heavenly bodies
Heterotroph hypothesis, SC-005-005
Hippocrates, SC-005-115
History and political science
  democratic societies (see Democratic societies)
  early civilizations (see Early civilizations)
  "enemy,"·definition and analysis, SS-010-205
  foreign policy decisions, SS-010-245
  human needs, meeting (see Human needs)
  international conflicts, political control over,
      SS-010-230, 235